# MASTERING ADOBE PREMIERE

## A Comprehensive Guide to Video Editing

Edwin Cano

*This book is dedicated to all the aspiring video editors, creative storytellers, and visual artists who strive to bring their visions to life through the power of Adobe Premiere Pro. Your passion and dedication to mastering the art of video editing inspire innovation and creativity in the world of digital media.*

*To the countless individuals who have shared their knowledge, offered their support, and contributed to the evolution of video editing, this guide is a testament to your influence and commitment.*

*And to everyone who embarks on this journey of learning and growth, may this book serve as a valuable resource in your pursuit of excellence and creativity.*

*"The best way to predict the future is to create it."*

— PETER DRUCKER

# CONTENTS

# INTRODUCTION

In today's digital age, video has become one of the most influential mediums for communication, storytelling, and expression. From engaging social media clips and informative YouTube videos to cinematic masterpieces and professional presentations, the art of video editing plays a pivotal role in shaping how we perceive and interact with content.

Adobe Premiere Pro is a leading video editing software that provides a powerful suite of tools for creating high-quality video content. Its versatility and advanced features make it the go-to choice for both amateur editors and industry professionals alike. Whether you're a budding filmmaker, a content creator, or a seasoned editor, mastering Premiere Pro can significantly enhance your ability to produce compelling and polished videos.

This book, Mastering Adobe Premiere Pro, is designed to be your comprehensive guide through the world of video editing with Adobe's flagship software. We will explore everything from the fundamental aspects of setting up your workspace to advanced editing techniques that can elevate your projects. Each chapter is crafted to build your skills progressively, ensuring a thorough understanding of Premiere Pro's capabilities.

What You'll Find Inside

Getting Started with Adobe Premiere Pro: Learn how to install and set up Premiere Pro, navigate its interface, and manage your projects efficiently.

Basic Editing Techniques: Understand how to navigate the timeline, cut and trim clips, and apply basic transitions to create a cohesive story.

Advanced Editing Tools: Delve into advanced features such as multi-camera editing, sequence management, and refined trimming techniques.

Audio Editing and Mixing: Discover how to manage, edit, and mix audio tracks to ensure professional-quality sound in your videos.

Adding and Customizing Effects: Explore how to apply and customize video effects, create animations with keyframes, and use LUTs for color correction.

Color Correction and Grading: Master the art of color correction and grading using the Lumetri Color panel to achieve the perfect look for your footage.

Titles and Graphics: Learn to create and edit titles, use graphics and templates, and animate text and graphics to enhance your video projects.

Exporting and Rendering: Understand the various export settings and rendering options to ensure your videos are optimized for different platforms and devices.

Workflow and Efficiency Tips: Discover tips and best practices for organizing media, using keyboard shortcuts, and collaborating effectively.

Troubleshooting and Common Issues: Address common

technical problems, optimize performance, and recover unsaved projects.

Real-World Project Examples: Walk through step-by-step examples of different types of video projects, including vlogs, short films, and documentaries.

Staying Current and Advanced Techniques: Explore how to keep up with software updates, new features, and industry trends to stay ahead of the curve.

Each section is filled with practical advice, illustrative examples, and hands-on exercises designed to enhance your learning experience. By the end of this guide, you will have a solid understanding of Adobe Premiere Pro's vast array of tools and techniques, empowering you to create videos that stand out in a crowded media landscape.

Whether you're looking to start a career in video editing or simply want to refine your skills, this book will be an invaluable resource on your journey to mastering Adobe Premiere Pro. Let's dive in and start exploring the exciting world of video editing!

# OVERVIEW OF ADOBE PREMIERE PRO

Adobe Premiere Pro is a professional video editing software used widely in film, television, and online media production. As part of Adobe's Creative Cloud suite, it provides an array of powerful tools and features designed for creating high-quality video content.

**Key Features:**

- **Non-Linear Editing (NLE):** Allows users to access and edit any part of their video without affecting other sections, providing flexibility and control.

- **Multi-Track Editing:** Supports multiple video and audio tracks, enabling complex projects with numerous layers of content.

- **High-Resolution Support:** Handles various resolutions, from standard HD to 4K and beyond, ensuring top-quality output.

- **Integration with Other Adobe Products:** Seamlessly integrates with tools like Adobe After Effects for motion graphics and Adobe Photoshop for image editing, enhancing workflow efficiency.

- **Extensive Format Compatibility:** Supports a wide range of file formats, making it versatile for different types of media and delivery requirements.

- **Advanced Color Grading and Correction:** Includes tools like the Lumetri Color panel for precise color adjustments and grading.

**Target Users:** Adobe Premiere Pro caters to a diverse audience, including:

- **Professional Editors:** Those working in film and television who require advanced editing capabilities.

- **Content Creators:** Individuals producing online videos, including YouTubers and vloggers, seeking high-quality production.

- **Marketing and Media Professionals:** Teams involved in creating promotional materials and multimedia content.

**Why Mastering Premiere Pro is Important:** Mastering Adobe Premiere Pro opens doors to creating polished, professional-level videos. Its extensive feature set and integration with other Adobe tools make it a powerful asset for achieving high production values and efficient workflows. This guide aims to equip users with the skills needed to harness Premiere Pro's full potential, whether for professional projects or personal creative endeavors.

# IMPORTANCE OF VIDEO EDITING SKILLS

In today's digital landscape, video editing skills are increasingly valuable across various industries. Whether for personal projects, professional work, or content creation, the ability to edit video effectively offers several significant advantages:

1. **Enhanced Communication:** Video is a powerful medium for conveying messages, stories, and ideas. Effective editing ensures clarity, coherence, and engagement, making it easier to communicate complex concepts and connect with audiences.

2. **Professionalism and Quality:** High-quality video content reflects professionalism. Skilled editing enhances the visual and audio elements of a video, contributing to a polished, professional final product that stands out in a crowded media environment.

3. **Creative Expression:** Video editing provides a platform for creativity. Editors can manipulate footage, apply effects, and craft narratives to express their unique vision and style, transforming raw material into compelling stories.

4. **Career Opportunities:** Proficiency in video editing opens up diverse career paths, from working in film and television to roles in marketing, advertising, and social media. It's a sought-after

skill in many fields, offering opportunities for freelance work or positions within organizations.

5. **Content Creation and Branding:** For entrepreneurs and businesses, video content is a key tool for branding and marketing. Effective video editing enhances promotional materials, advertisements, and social media content, helping to attract and retain customers.

6. **Improved Engagement:** Well-edited videos are more engaging and likely to hold viewers' attention. By cutting unnecessary parts, adding dynamic elements, and ensuring smooth transitions, editors can create content that captivates and maintains audience interest.

7. **Versatility and Adaptability:** Video editing skills are adaptable to various formats and platforms. Whether for YouTube, social media, corporate presentations, or educational materials, the ability to tailor content to different needs and specifications is crucial.

8. **Problem-Solving:** Video editing often involves troubleshooting and solving technical challenges. Developing these skills enhances one's ability to address issues creatively and effectively, which is valuable in any media-related role.

In summary, mastering video editing skills not only enhances the quality of video content but also opens up numerous professional opportunities and enables creative expression. Whether for personal projects or professional work, effective editing is essential for producing impactful and engaging videos.

# GOALS OF THE GUIDE

The primary goals of this guide, "Mastering Adobe Premiere Pro," are designed to ensure readers gain comprehensive knowledge and practical skills in using the software effectively. Here's a breakdown of the key objectives:

1. **Provide a Comprehensive Understanding of Adobe Premiere Pro:**

   - Introduce the software's interface, features, and tools.
   - Explain the core concepts and functionalities of video editing within Premiere Pro.

2. **Develop Practical Editing Skills:**

   - Teach fundamental editing techniques, including cutting, trimming, and sequencing.
   - Offer advanced editing methods such as multi-camera editing and complex transitions.

3. **Enhance Audio and Visual Quality:**

   - Guide readers through audio editing and mixing to ensure clear and balanced sound.
   - Demonstrate techniques for color correction and grading to improve the visual appeal of videos.

## 4. **Incorporate Effects and Graphics:**

- Show how to apply and customize effects, transitions, and graphics.
- Introduce title creation, text animation, and integration with other Adobe tools like After Effects.

## 5. **Master Exporting and Rendering:**

- Provide detailed instructions on exporting projects in various formats for different platforms.
- Explain rendering options to ensure high-quality output.

## 6. **Optimize Workflow and Efficiency:**

- Share tips for organizing media, using keyboard shortcuts, and customizing the workspace.
- Offer strategies for streamlining the editing process and managing complex projects.

## 7. **Address Common Challenges and Troubleshooting:**

- Identify and solve common issues encountered during editing.
- Provide solutions for optimizing performance and recovering projects.

## 8. **Illustrate Real-World Applications:**

- Present practical examples and case studies to demonstrate how the techniques and tools are applied in real-world scenarios.
- Provide project walkthroughs to give hands-on experience.

## 9. **Prepare for Continued Learning and Growth:**

- Encourage readers to stay current with software updates and industry trends.

- Offer resources for further learning and exploration of advanced techniques.

By achieving these goals, the guide aims to equip readers with the skills and knowledge necessary to excel in video editing using Adobe Premiere Pro, whether they are beginners or seeking to refine their expertise.

# CHAPTER 1:
# GETTING STARTED
# WITH ADOBE
# PREMIERE PRO

# INSTALLING AND SETTING UP PREMIERE PRO

**1**. System Requirements and Compatibility:

- **Hardware Requirements:** Ensure your computer meets Adobe Premiere Pro's minimum hardware specifications, including processor speed, RAM, and graphics card capabilities.

- **Software Requirements:** Check for compatible operating systems (Windows or macOS) and any necessary software updates.

2. **Subscription and Download:**

- **Adobe Creative Cloud Subscription:** Purchase a subscription to Adobe Creative Cloud, which provides access to Premiere Pro and other Adobe applications.

- **Downloading the Software:**
  - Visit the Adobe Creative Cloud website or use the Creative Cloud Desktop app.
  - Sign in with your Adobe ID and download Premiere Pro from the app or the Adobe

website.

## 3. Installation Process:

- **Running the Installer:**
  - Locate the downloaded installer file and double-click to start the installation process.
  - Follow the on-screen instructions to install Premiere Pro on your computer.

- **Choosing Installation Options:**
  - Select the installation location (default or custom).
  - Choose additional options, if available, such as creating shortcuts or installing additional components.

## 4. Initial Setup and Configuration:

- **Launching Premiere Pro:**
  - Open Premiere Pro from the Applications folder (macOS) or Start Menu (Windows).
  - Sign in with your Adobe ID if prompted.

- **Workspace Setup:**
  - Familiarize yourself with the default workspace layout, including the Project panel, Timeline, Program Monitor, and Source Monitor.
  - Customize your workspace by rearranging panels or choosing from preset workspace layouts (Editing, Assembly, Color, etc.).

- **Creating a New Project:**
  - Click on "New Project" from the Welcome screen or File menu.
  - Enter a project name and choose a save location.

◦ Configure project settings, including video and audio settings, depending on your project requirements.

## 5. Importing Media:

- **Adding Media to Your Project:**
  ◦ Use the "Import" option from the File menu or drag and drop files directly into the Project panel.

  ◦ Organize your media in bins (folders) to keep your project structured.

- **Understanding Media Management:**
  ◦ Learn how to manage media files, including their location and metadata, to ensure smooth editing and avoid missing files.

## 6. Getting Acquainted with the Interface:

- **Navigating the Interface:**
  ◦ Explore the key panels: Project, Source Monitor, Timeline, Program Monitor, and Effects.

  ◦ Learn the purpose and function of each panel to understand their roles in the editing process.

- **Customizing the Workspace:**
  ◦ Adjust the layout of panels to suit your workflow preferences.

  ◦ Save custom workspace arrangements for future use.

## 7. Setting Up Preferences:

- **Configuring General Preferences:**
  ◦ Access preferences from the Edit menu (Windows) or Premiere Pro menu (macOS).

- Adjust settings for general operation, appearance, and performance according to your needs.

- **Setting Up Keyboard Shortcuts:**
    - Customize keyboard shortcuts to streamline your editing workflow.
    - Access shortcut settings from the Edit menu (Windows) or Premiere Pro menu (macOS).

By following these steps, you'll be prepared to start editing with Adobe Premiere Pro, with a solid foundation in the software's installation, setup, and initial configuration.

# UNDERSTANDING
# THE INTERFACE

# WORKSPACE LAYOUT

Adobe Premiere Pro's interface is designed to streamline the video editing process, offering various panels and tools that can be customized to suit your workflow. Here's a detailed look at the workspace layout and its components:

1. **Main Panels:**

- **Project Panel:**
  - **Purpose:** Acts as the central hub for managing and organizing all your media assets, including video clips, audio files, images, and sequences.
  - **Features:** Includes bins (folders) for categorizing media, metadata display, and search functionality.

- **Source Monitor:**
  - **Purpose:** Allows you to preview and trim your media clips before adding them to the timeline.
  - **Features:** Includes controls for play/pause, marking in and out points, and setting playback options.

- **Timeline Panel:**

- **Purpose:** The primary area for assembling and editing your media. You can arrange clips, add transitions, and apply effects.
- **Features:** Displays multiple tracks for video and audio, with tools for cutting, moving, and adjusting clips.

- **Program Monitor:**
  - **Purpose:** Displays the output of your edited sequence, showing how your project looks after applying edits.
  - **Features:** Includes playback controls, resolution settings, and options for full-screen viewing.

- **Effects Panel:**
  - **Purpose:** Contains various video and audio effects, transitions, and presets that you can apply to your clips.
  - **Features:** Organizes effects into categories for easy access and customization.

- **Tools Panel:**
  - **Purpose:** Provides access to essential editing tools, such as the Selection Tool, Razor Tool, and Type Tool.
  - **Features:** Includes icons for each tool, allowing quick selection and application.

## 2. Workspace Customization:

- **Arranging Panels:**
  - You can rearrange panels by dragging and dropping them to different areas of the workspace.
  - Create custom layouts by resizing, docking, or floating panels according to your preferences.

- **Saving Workspaces:**
  - After customizing your workspace, save your layout by going to the Window menu > Workspaces > Save as New Workspace.
  - This allows you to quickly switch between different layouts for various editing tasks.

- **Workspace Presets:**
  - Premiere Pro offers several workspace presets (e.g., Editing, Color, Audio) tailored for different editing needs.
  - Switch between presets by going to the Window menu > Workspaces and selecting the desired layout.

## 3. Additional Interface Features:

- **Menu Bar:**
  - Located at the top of the screen, it provides access to various tools, preferences, and commands (e.g., File, Edit, Sequence).

- **Toolbar:**
  - Found on the left side of the workspace, it includes tools for editing, navigating, and creating content (e.g., Selection Tool, Hand Tool).

- **Panels and Tabs:**
  - Most panels can be expanded, collapsed, or docked as tabs within the workspace, allowing for flexible arrangement.

- **Audio Meters:**
  - Display real-time audio levels for monitoring and adjusting audio during playback.

## 4. Workspace Management:

- **Resetting Workspaces:**
  - If your workspace becomes disorganized or you want to revert to the default layout, go to the Window menu > Workspaces > Reset to Saved Layout.

- **Workspace Switching:**
  - Quickly switch between different workspaces based on your editing needs by selecting from the workspace presets in the Window menu.

Understanding and customizing the workspace layout in Adobe Premiere Pro is essential for an efficient editing workflow. Familiarizing yourself with each panel and its functions will help streamline your editing process and improve productivity.

# PANELS AND TOOLS

Adobe Premiere Pro's interface includes several key panels and tools essential for video editing. Each component serves a specific function, providing a range of capabilities for managing and editing your media. Here's a detailed overview of the primary panels and tools:

1. **Project Panel:**

- **Function:** Central hub for managing media assets and project organization.

- **Features:**
  - **Bins:** Organizational folders for sorting media files.
  - **Media Browser:** Tool for navigating and importing media from your file system.
  - **Metadata:** Displays information about selected clips, such as file format, duration, and frame rate.
  - **Search and Filter Options:** Find specific files quickly within the project.

2. **Source Monitor:**

- **Function:** Preview and trim clips before adding them to the timeline.

- **Features:**
  - **Playback Controls:** Play, pause, rewind, and fast forward your clips.
  - **In/Out Points:** Mark the start and end points of the clip for trimming or inserting into the timeline.
  - **Clip Information:** View details about the selected clip, such as frame rate and duration.

## 3. Timeline Panel:

- **Function:** The main area for arranging and editing media clips.
- **Features:**
  - **Tracks:** Separate video and audio tracks where you place and organize clips.
  - **Timeline Ruler:** Displays timecode and helps with precise placement and editing.
  - **Tools:** For cutting, moving, and adjusting clips.
  - **Markers:** Add markers to indicate specific points or notes within your sequence.

## 4. Program Monitor:

- **Function:** Displays the final output of your edited sequence.
- **Features:**
  - **Playback Controls:** Play, pause, and scrub through your edited sequence.
  - **Resolution Settings:** Adjust playback resolution to fit your needs (e.g., Full, 1/2, 1/4).
  - **Safe Margins and Guides:** Visual aids for

ensuring content is properly framed for different screen sizes.

## 5. Effects Panel:

- **Function:** Access and apply video and audio effects to your clips.

- **Features:**
    - **Effect Categories:** Organize effects into categories like Color Correction, Blur & Sharpen, and Transitions.
    - **Effect Presets:** Predefined settings for quickly applying popular effects.
    - **Search Function:** Find specific effects and presets by name.

## 6. Tools Panel:

- **Function:** Provides essential tools for editing and creating content.

- **Features:**
    - **Selection Tool:** For selecting and moving clips.
    - **Razor Tool:** For cutting clips into segments.
    - **Type Tool:** For adding text and titles to your project.
    - **Hand Tool:** For navigating the timeline and program monitor.

## 7. Audio Meters:

- **Function:** Monitor audio levels during playback.

- **Features:**
    - **Level Indicators:** Show real-time audio levels to help with balancing and mixing.
    - **Peak Hold:** Displays maximum audio levels reached during playback.

## 8. Effects Controls Panel:

- **Function:** Adjust settings for applied effects and transitions.
- **Features:**
  - **Effect Parameters:** Modify specific settings of applied effects, such as opacity, position, and scale.
  - **Keyframes:** Animate effect properties over time using keyframes.

## 9. Lumetri Color Panel:

- **Function:** Perform color correction and grading.
- **Features:**
  - **Basic Correction:** Adjust exposure, contrast, highlights, and shadows.
  - **Creative:** Apply LUTs and color presets.
  - **Curves and Color Wheels:** Fine-tune color balance and grading.

## 10. Essential Graphics Panel:

- **Function:** Create and edit text and graphics.
- **Features:**
  - **Text Tools:** Design titles, captions, and other text elements.
  - **Graphics Templates:** Use and customize pre-designed templates.

By familiarizing yourself with these panels and tools, you'll be able to navigate Adobe Premiere Pro more effectively and utilize its full range of editing capabilities. Each component plays a crucial role in the video editing process, allowing you to manage, edit, and enhance your media efficiently.

# PROJECT CREATION

# SETTING UP A
# NEW PROJECT

C reating a new project in Adobe Premiere Pro is the first step in starting your video editing work. Properly setting up your project ensures that your media is organized and that the editing process runs smoothly. Here's a step-by-step guide to setting up a new project:

1. **Launching Premiere Pro:**

   - Open Adobe Premiere Pro from your Applications folder (macOS) or Start Menu (Windows).

   - If prompted, sign in with your Adobe ID.

2. **Starting a New Project:**

   - On the Welcome screen, click on "New Project." Alternatively, you can go to the File menu and select "New" > "Project."

3. **Project Settings Dialog Box:**

   - **Project Name:**
     - Enter a descriptive name for your project. This helps in identifying and locating the project file later.

   - **Location:**

- ◦ Click on "Browse" to choose a save location for your project file. It's advisable to store the project file and media in the same folder for organization.

- **Ingest Settings:**
  - ◦ If you need to ingest (import and process) media, enable the Ingest checkbox. You can configure additional ingest settings by clicking on the wrench icon.

## 4. Setting Up Ingest Presets (Optional):

- **Ingest Presets:**
  - ◦ Click the wrench icon next to the Ingest checkbox to configure ingest settings.
  - ◦ Choose an ingest preset or create a new one if you need to transcode media to a different format or create proxies.

## 5. Selecting Video and Audio Settings:

- **General Settings:**
  - ◦ **Renderer:** Choose the rendering engine (e.g., Mercury Playback Engine GPU Acceleration) based on your system's capabilities.
  - ◦ **Display Format:** Set the timecode display format (e.g., Timecode, Frames).

- **Scratch Disks:**
  - ◦ Configure the locations for scratch disks where Premiere Pro stores temporary files, including video previews, audio previews, and project autosave files. It's a good practice to set these to separate drives for better performance.

## 6. Sequence Settings (Optional):

- You can set up sequence settings during project

creation or later when creating a new sequence.

- **Creating a New Sequence:**
  - ◦ After setting up the project, go to the File menu > New > Sequence, or use the New Item button in the Project panel.
  - ◦ Choose a sequence preset that matches your media format or customize your sequence settings as needed.

## 7. Importing Media:

- **Import Media:**
  - ◦ Use the "Import" option from the File menu, or drag and drop media files directly into the Project panel.
  - ◦ Organize your media in bins within the Project panel to keep your project structured.

## 8. Saving Your Project:

- **Initial Save:**
  - ◦ Click "Save" or use the shortcut Ctrl+S (Cmd+S on macOS) to save your project file.
  - ◦ Regularly save your project to avoid losing progress and enable auto-save features from the Preferences menu.

By carefully setting up your project, you establish a solid foundation for efficient and organized video editing. This setup process ensures that your media is correctly managed and that your editing environment is tailored to your specific needs.

# IMPORTING MEDIA

Importing media into Adobe Premiere Pro is a crucial step in beginning your video editing project. This process allows you to bring video, audio, and image files into your project so you can use them in your sequences. Here's how to import media effectively:

1. **Using the Media Browser:**

- **Accessing the Media Browser:**
  - Open the Media Browser by selecting it from the Window menu or clicking the Media Browser tab if it's already visible in your workspace.

- **Navigating to Media Files:**
  - Browse your computer or connected drives to locate the media files you want to import.
  - The Media Browser provides a directory view and previews of your files, making it easy to select and import them.

- **Importing Files:**
  - Right-click on the desired files or folders and select "Import."
  - Alternatively, drag and drop files directly into the Project panel from the Media Browser.

## 2. Using the Import Dialog Box:

- **Accessing Import:**
  - Go to the File menu and select "Import," or use the shortcut Ctrl+I (Cmd+I on macOS).

- **Selecting Files:**
  - In the dialog box that opens, navigate to the location of your media files.
  - Select the files or folders you want to import and click "Open."

- **Importing Folders:**
  - If you import a folder, Premiere Pro will create a bin in the Project panel with the same name as the folder and import all files within it.

## 3. Drag and Drop:

- **Direct Import:**
  - Drag media files directly from your file explorer or desktop into the Project panel.
  - Drop the files into the desired bin or into the empty space within the Project panel.

## 4. Organizing Media:

- **Creating Bins:**
  - Organize your media by creating bins (folders) within the Project panel. Right-click in the Project panel and select "New Bin" or use the New Bin button.

- **Naming and Structuring:**
  - Name bins according to media types or project sections (e.g., "Footage," "Audio," "Graphics") for better organization.

## 5. Media Management:

- **Relinking Media:**

- If you move or rename media files outside of Premiere Pro, you may need to relink them. Right-click the missing media in the Project panel and select "Link Media" to locate and reconnect the files.

- **Creating Proxies (Optional):**
    - For smoother editing with high-resolution files, consider creating proxies. Ingest settings allow you to automatically create lower-resolution versions of your media for easier editing.

## 6. Import Settings and Preferences:

- **Preferences:**
    - Adjust import preferences from the Edit menu (Windows) or Premiere Pro menu (macOS) > Preferences > Media.

    - Configure settings for how Premiere Pro handles media import, including audio and video file handling.

By effectively importing and organizing your media, you create a streamlined workflow that enhances productivity and helps maintain project organization. Proper media management is key to a smooth editing experience and successful project outcomes.

# CHAPTER 2: BASIC EDITING TECHNIQUES

# NAVIGATING THE TIMELINE

The Timeline panel in Adobe Premiere Pro is where the bulk of video editing takes place. Understanding how to navigate and use the Timeline efficiently is crucial for organizing and editing your media. Here's a detailed guide on how to navigate the Timeline:

1. **Timeline Overview:**

- **Tracks:**
  - **Video Tracks:** Display video clips, graphics, and effects. Tracks are stacked vertically, and you can have multiple video tracks to layer clips.
  - **Audio Tracks:** Display audio clips, voiceovers, and sound effects. Audio tracks are also stacked vertically, with each track representing a separate audio channel.

- **Timeline Ruler:**
  - Displays timecode and helps with precise placement of clips. The ruler shows the duration of the sequence and helps in managing the timing of edits.

2. **Scrolling and Zooming:**

- **Scrolling Horizontally:**
  - Use the horizontal scroll bar at the bottom of the Timeline panel or swipe left/right on your mouse or trackpad to move through the sequence.

- **Zooming In and Out:**
  - **Zoom Slider:** Use the zoom slider at the bottom of the Timeline panel to adjust the level of detail in the Timeline view.
  - **Keyboard Shortcuts:** Use the "+" (plus) key to zoom in and the "–" (minus) key to zoom out.
  - **Mouse Scroll:** Hold the Alt key (Option key on macOS) and scroll with your mouse wheel to zoom in and out on the Timeline.

3. **Navigating Clips:**

- **Selecting Clips:**
  - Click on a clip in the Timeline to select it. You can select multiple clips by holding down the Shift key while clicking.

- **Moving Clips:**
  - Drag and drop clips to reposition them on the Timeline. Ensure you're placing them on the correct track to avoid overlap issues.

- **Trimming Clips:**
  - Hover over the edges of a clip until the Trim Tool appears. Drag the edge to adjust the clip's in and out points.

4. **Using Markers:**

- **Adding Markers:**
  - Press the "M" key to add a marker at the current playhead position. Markers can be used to label key points or make notes.

- **Navigating to Markers:**
  - Use the marker navigation buttons (Next Marker, Previous Marker) or use the marker list to jump to specific markers in the Timeline.

## 5. Using the Playhead and Playback Controls:

- **Playhead:**
  - The playhead is a vertical line that indicates the current position in the Timeline. Drag it to move through your sequence.

- **Playback Controls:**
  - Use the playback controls (Play, Pause, Stop) located in the Program Monitor to play or pause your sequence. You can also use the spacebar to toggle playback.

## 6. Adding and Removing Tracks:

- **Adding Tracks:**
  - Right-click in the empty area of the Timeline or use the Timeline panel menu to select "Add Track." Choose either a Video Track or Audio Track.

- **Removing Tracks:**
  - Right-click on the track header and select "Delete Track" or use the Timeline panel menu to remove unwanted tracks.

## 7. Adjusting Track Height and Visibility:

- **Track Height:**
  - Adjust the height of individual tracks by dragging the track borders up or down. This can help in better viewing of clip details and editing precision.

- **Track Visibility:**
  - Use the eye icons next to the track headers to

toggle the visibility of video tracks. For audio, use the speaker icons to mute/unmute tracks.

## 8. Navigating Sequences:

- **Multiple Sequences:**
  - Manage multiple sequences by selecting them from the Project panel. Double-click a sequence to open it in the Timeline panel.

- **Sequence Tabs:**
  - If you have multiple sequences open, they will appear as tabs in the Timeline panel. Click on the tabs to switch between different sequences.

Understanding how to navigate and utilize the Timeline effectively will significantly improve your efficiency in editing and help you achieve precise and organized results.

# CUTTING AND TRIMMING CLIPS

Cutting and trimming clips are fundamental editing techniques used to refine your video, remove unwanted sections, and adjust the timing of your content. Here's how to perform these tasks in Adobe Premiere Pro:

1. **Cutting Clips:**

- **Using the Razor Tool:**
    - **Selecting the Razor Tool:** Click on the Razor Tool (or press the "C" key) in the Tools panel. The cursor will change to a razor blade icon.

    - **Cutting Clips:** Click on the clip at the desired point in the Timeline to create a cut. The clip will be split into two separate segments at the cut point.

    - **Adjusting Cuts:** After cutting, you can move or delete individual segments as needed.

- **Using the Playhead for Cutting:**
    - **Position the Playhead:** Move the playhead to the point where you want to cut the clip.

    - **Cutting with Keyboard Shortcuts:** Select the clip, then use the "Ctrl+K" (Cmd+K on macOS) shortcut to cut the clip at the playhead position.

- **Using the Razor Blade Icon:**
  - ○ **Activating Razor Blade:** Hold down the "Alt" key (Option key on macOS) while clicking on the clip in the Timeline to make a cut.

## 2. Trimming Clips:

- **Trimming with the Selection Tool:**
  - ○ **Selecting the Selection Tool:** Click on the Selection Tool (or press the "V" key) in the Tools panel.

  - ○ **Trimming Edges:** Hover over the beginning or end of a clip in the Timeline until you see the trim handle (a red bracket). Click and drag the handle to trim the clip's duration.

  - ○ **Live Preview:** As you trim, you can preview the changes in the Program Monitor to ensure you're trimming to the desired point.

- **Trimming in the Source Monitor:**
  - ○ **Opening a Clip in Source Monitor:** Double-click on the clip in the Project panel to open it in the Source Monitor.

  - ○ **Setting In and Out Points:** Use the Mark In (I) and Mark Out (O) buttons to define the portion of the clip you want to use.

  - ○ **Dragging to Timeline:** Drag the trimmed portion from the Source Monitor to the Timeline.

- **Ripple Edit Tool:**
  - ○ **Selecting the Ripple Edit Tool:** Click on the Ripple Edit Tool (or press the "B" key) in the Tools panel.

- ○ **Trimming with Ripple Edit:** Click and drag the edge of a clip to trim it. The Ripple Edit Tool automatically adjusts the position of subsequent clips to fill the gap created by the trim.

- **Rolling Edit Tool:**
  - ○ **Selecting the Rolling Edit Tool:** Click on the Rolling Edit Tool (or press the "N" key) in the Tools panel.

  - ○ **Adjusting Edit Points:** Click and drag the edit point between two clips. This will adjust the in and out points of adjacent clips without affecting the overall duration of the sequence.

3. **Adjusting Clip Duration and Playback:**

- **Duration Display:**
  - ○ Check the duration of trimmed clips by looking at the clip's length displayed in the Timeline or in the Program Monitor.

- **Playback Controls:**
  - ○ Use playback controls to review the edited sequence and ensure that the cutting and trimming are accurate.

4. **Using Trim Mode (Advanced):**

- **Entering Trim Mode:**
  - ○ Select a clip and press "T" to enter Trim Mode.

  - ○ Use the Trim Mode tools to make precise adjustments to the clip's in and out points while viewing the changes in real time.

- **Adjusting Edits:**
  - ○ Use the Trim Mode's controls to fine-tune your edits, adjust the duration of clips, and review how changes affect the sequence.

By mastering cutting and trimming techniques, you can effectively refine your video, remove unnecessary content, and ensure that your edits are smooth and well-timed.

# BASIC TRANSITIONS

Transitions in Adobe Premiere Pro help to create smooth visual connections between clips, adding polish and continuity to your video. Here's how to use basic transitions effectively:

1. **Applying Transitions:**

- **Accessing Transitions:**
  - Open the Effects panel by going to Window > Effects or selecting it from the workspace if it's visible.
  - Navigate to the "Video Transitions" folder to view available transition categories (e.g., Dissolve, Wipe, Slide).

- **Choosing a Transition:**
  - Browse through the transition categories and select the desired transition effect.

- **Applying the Transition:**
  - **Drag and Drop:** Drag the chosen transition effect from the Effects panel and drop it between two clips on the Timeline.
  - **Double-Click:** Alternatively, you can double-click the transition effect to apply it automatically to the edit point between clips.

## 2. Adjusting Transition Duration:

- **Adjusting Duration in the Timeline:**
  - ○ **Select the Transition:** Click on the transition effect in the Timeline to select it.
  - ○ **Resize the Transition:** Drag the edges of the transition to adjust its duration. Shortening or lengthening the transition will affect how quickly or slowly the effect occurs.

- **Adjusting Duration in the Effect Controls Panel:**
  - ○ **Open Effect Controls Panel:** Go to Window > Effect Controls or select it from the workspace.
  - ○ **Modify Duration:** Find the transition effect in the Effect Controls panel and adjust the duration by entering a new time value.

## 3. Customizing Transition Effects:

- **Transition Settings:**
  - ○ **Select the Transition:** Click on the transition in the Timeline or Effect Controls panel.
  - ○ **Adjust Settings:** Use the Effect Controls panel to modify transition parameters. Some transitions allow you to adjust properties like direction, border width, or angle.

- **Previewing Transitions:**
  - ○ **Playhead Preview:** Move the playhead over the transition area and use playback controls to preview how the transition looks in your sequence.
  - ○ **Adjust as Needed:** Based on the preview, make additional adjustments to achieve the desired effect.

## 4. Common Basic Transitions:

- **Cross Dissolve:**
  - **Description:** Creates a gradual fade from one clip to the next, often used for smooth scene changes.
  - **Application:** Drag the Cross Dissolve transition between clips for a standard dissolve effect.
- **Dip to Black/Dip to White:**
  - **Description:** Fades to black or white between clips, commonly used for dramatic scene changes or transitions.
  - **Application:** Apply the Dip to Black or Dip to White transition to create a fade effect.
- **Wipe:**
  - **Description:** Moves one clip out of view while bringing the next clip into view, often with a directional wipe.
  - **Application:** Apply the Wipe transition and customize the direction or shape of the wipe.
- **Slide:**
  - **Description:** Slides the incoming clip over the outgoing clip, creating a dynamic transition effect.
  - **Application:** Use the Slide transition to add a sliding effect between clips.

5. **Transition Effects Tips:**

- **Use Sparingly:** Avoid overusing transitions. Use them strategically to enhance the narrative or visual appeal of your video.
- **Match Transitions to Content:** Choose transitions that fit the style and tone of your video. For example, use

smoother transitions for dramatic scenes and more dynamic ones for action sequences.

- **Consistency:** Maintain consistency in the use of transitions throughout your video to create a cohesive look and feel.

By applying and customizing basic transitions, you can enhance the flow and visual appeal of your video, making it more engaging for your audience.

# ADDING AND MANAGING CLIPS ON THE TIMELINE

Managing clips on the Timeline is essential for organizing your project, sequencing your content, and achieving a polished final product. Here's how to effectively add and manage clips in Adobe Premiere Pro:

1. **Adding Clips to the Timeline:**

- **Dragging Clips from the Project Panel:**
  - **Open the Project Panel:** Make sure your media files are imported and visible in the Project panel.

  - **Drag and Drop:** Click and drag a clip from the Project panel directly onto the Timeline. Position it on the desired video or audio track.

- **Using the Source Monitor:**
  - **Open a Clip:** Double-click a clip in the Project panel to open it in the Source Monitor.

  - **Set In and Out Points:** Use the Mark In (I) and Mark Out (O) buttons to select the portion of the clip you want to use.

- **Drag to Timeline:** Drag the selected portion from the Source Monitor to the Timeline. Drop it on the desired track and position.

- **Using the Insert and Overwrite Buttons:**
  - **Insert Button:** Click the Insert button (or press ",") to insert the selected clip from the Source Monitor into the Timeline at the current playhead position. This pushes existing clips to the right.
  - **Overwrite Button:** Click the Overwrite button (or press ".") to replace the selected area in the Timeline with the clip from the Source Monitor without pushing existing clips.

2. **Managing Clips on the Timeline:**

- **Selecting and Moving Clips:**
  - **Selecting Clips:** Click on a clip to select it. Hold Shift to select multiple clips.
  - **Moving Clips:** Drag the selected clip(s) to a new position on the Timeline. Ensure you place them on the correct track and avoid overlapping unless intentional.

- **Aligning Clips:**
  - **Snap to Timeline:** Enable snapping by clicking the Snap tool (magnet icon) or pressing the "S" key. This helps align clips to the playhead or other clips.
  - **Manual Alignment:** Drag clips manually to align with other clips or markers if snapping is not required.

- **Cutting and Trimming Clips:**
  - **Cutting:** Use the Razor Tool (C) to split clips into segments at specific points. This allows

for removing or rearranging sections.

- **Trimming:** Use the Selection Tool (V) to adjust the in and out points of clips by dragging the edges. This modifies the duration and content of the clip.

- **Copying and Pasting Clips:**
  - **Copying:** Select the clip(s) and use Ctrl+C (Cmd +C on macOS) to copy.
  - **Pasting:** Move the playhead to the desired position and use Ctrl+V (Cmd+V on macOS) to paste the copied clip(s) onto the Timeline.

- **Duplicating Clips:**
  - **Duplicate:** Hold the Alt key (Option key on macOS) while dragging the clip to create a duplicate copy on the Timeline.

- **Deleting Clips:**
  - **Select and Delete:** Click on the clip to select it, then press the Delete key or right-click and choose "Clear" to remove it from the Timeline.

3. **Adjusting Clip Properties:**

- **Clip Length and Speed:**
  - **Speed/Duration:** Right-click on a clip and select "Speed/Duration" to change the speed or duration of the clip.
  - **Time Stretching:** Drag the edge of the clip while holding down the Alt key (Option key on macOS) to stretch or compress the clip duration.

- **Clip Effects:**
  - **Apply Effects:** Use the Effects panel to drag and drop effects onto clips in the Timeline.
  - **Adjust Effects:** Use the Effect Controls panel to

tweak effect parameters applied to the clip.

## 4. Using Markers:

- **Adding Markers:** Press the "M" key to add markers to the Timeline, which can help identify key points or make notes.

- **Navigating Markers:** Use marker navigation buttons or the marker list to jump to specific markers.

## 5. Organizing Tracks:

- **Renaming Tracks:** Double-click on the track name to rename it for better organization (e.g., "B-Roll," "Voiceover").

- **Locking and Hiding Tracks:** Use the lock icon to prevent accidental changes and the eye icon to hide or show tracks.

By effectively adding and managing clips on the Timeline, you ensure that your video editing process is organized and efficient, leading to a smoother editing workflow and a well-structured final project.

# CHAPTER 3: ADVANCED EDITING TOOLS

# USING THE RAZOR TOOL

The Razor Tool in Adobe Premiere Pro is essential for precise cutting of clips on the Timeline. It allows you to split clips into segments, making it easier to rearrange, delete, or modify parts of your footage. Here's a comprehensive guide on using the Razor Tool:

1. **Accessing the Razor Tool:**

   - **Tool Panel:**
     - **Selecting the Razor Tool:** Click on the Razor Tool icon (a razor blade) in the Tools panel, or press the "C" key on your keyboard to activate it.

     - **Keyboard Shortcut:** Press "C" to switch to the Razor Tool, and press "V" to return to the Selection Tool.

   - **Contextual Use:**
     - **Tool Context:** The Razor Tool can be used within the Timeline to cut clips. Ensure you're in the correct sequence view where you want to make cuts.

2. **Making Cuts:**

- **Single Cut:**
  - **Positioning the Playhead:** Move the playhead to the point where you want to cut the clip.
  - **Applying the Cut:** Click directly on the clip at the playhead position. The clip will be split into two segments at that point.

- **Multiple Cuts:**
  - **Click and Drag:** Click and drag the Razor Tool across multiple clips to make cuts across all selected clips.
  - **Multiple Selection:** If you want to cut multiple clips, hold the Shift key and click to select multiple clips, then use the Razor Tool.

3. **Adjusting Cuts:**

- **Cutting Multiple Clips:**
  - **Across Tracks:** To cut clips across multiple video or audio tracks, simply drag the Razor Tool across the tracks. All clips intersected by the drag will be cut.

- **Undoing Cuts:**
  - **Undo Command:** If you make a cut by mistake, press Ctrl+Z (Cmd+Z on macOS) to undo the last action.

4. **Using the Razor Tool in Different Modes:**

- **Regular Cut:**
  - **Standard Use:** Click on a clip or across clips to create standard cuts at specific points.

- **Targeted Cuts:**
  - **Active Track:** Ensure the correct track is active (highlighted) when making cuts. The Razor Tool will cut only on the active track if multiple tracks are present.

## 5. Fine-Tuning Cuts:

- **Zoom In for Precision:**
  - **Timeline Zoom:** Use the zoom slider or keyboard shortcuts (Alt+scroll wheel) to zoom in on the Timeline for more precise cuts.

- **Adjusting Segments:**
  - **Selection Tool:** After cutting, use the Selection Tool (V) to move or delete the new segments as needed.

## 6. Combining with Other Tools:

- **Ripple Edit Tool:**
  - **Adjusting Cuts:** After making cuts with the Razor Tool, use the Ripple Edit Tool (B) to close gaps or adjust the timing of adjacent clips.

- **Rolling Edit Tool:**
  - **Fine-Tuning Edits:** Use the Rolling Edit Tool (N) to adjust the in and out points of adjacent clips without changing the overall sequence duration.

## 7. Practical Tips:

- **Use Labels and Markers:**
  - **Labeling Clips:** Label clips or add markers before cutting to keep track of important points in your footage.

- **Organize Clips Post-Cut:**
  - **Rearrange Segments:** After cutting, organize the resulting segments by dragging them to new positions or inserting new clips between cuts.

- **Regular Saves:**
  - **Save Frequently:** Regularly save your project to avoid losing changes made with the Razor

Tool.

Mastering the Razor Tool allows for precise and efficient editing, enabling you to refine your footage and achieve the desired results in your video projects.

# ADVANCED TRIMMING TECHNIQUES

Advanced trimming techniques in Adobe Premiere Pro provide greater control over your video's timing and flow, allowing for precise edits and seamless transitions. Here's how to employ these techniques effectively:

1. **Ripple Edit Tool:**

- **Purpose:**
  - The Ripple Edit Tool (B) adjusts the duration of a clip and automatically shifts subsequent clips to fill the gap or extend the sequence.

- **Using the Ripple Edit Tool:**
  - **Select the Tool:** Click on the Ripple Edit Tool in the Tools panel or press "B" on your keyboard.
  - **Trimming with Ripple Edit:** Hover over the edge of the clip until you see the Ripple Edit icon. Click and drag to adjust the clip's in or out point. The adjacent clips will move accordingly, maintaining the sequence's continuity.

- **Applications:**
  - Use for quick adjustments to clip lengths while

keeping your sequence synchronized.

## 2. Rolling Edit Tool:

- **Purpose:**
  - The Rolling Edit Tool (N) adjusts the in and out points of two adjacent clips simultaneously without affecting the overall length of the sequence.

- **Using the Rolling Edit Tool:**
  - **Select the Tool:** Click on the Rolling Edit Tool in the Tools panel or press "N" on your keyboard.
  - **Adjusting Edits:** Hover over the edit point between two clips. Click and drag left or right to adjust the in and out points of both clips. This technique allows for smooth transitions without altering the sequence's overall duration.

- **Applications:**
  - Ideal for fine-tuning transitions between clips and adjusting timing without creating gaps or overlaps.

## 3. Slip and Slide Edits:

- **Slip Edit:**
  - **Purpose:** The Slip Edit Tool (Y) changes the in and out points of a clip while keeping the clip's position on the Timeline unchanged.
  - **Using the Slip Edit Tool:** Click on the Slip Tool in the Tools panel or press "Y." Click and drag the clip to adjust its content while maintaining its duration and position.

- **Slide Edit:**
  - **Purpose:** The Slide Edit Tool (U) moves a

clip along the Timeline while adjusting the adjacent clips to accommodate the movement, thereby keeping the sequence duration constant.

- **Using the Slide Edit Tool:** Click on the Slide Tool in the Tools panel or press "U." Click and drag the clip to slide it along the Timeline. The adjacent clips will adjust to fit the new position.

## 4. Trim Mode:

- **Purpose:**
  - Trim Mode allows for precise trimming of clip edges and transitions using real-time visual feedback.

- **Entering Trim Mode:**
  - **Access Trim Mode:** Select a clip and press "T" on your keyboard to enter Trim Mode. The Program Monitor will display the Trim Mode interface.

- **Using Trim Mode:**
  - **Adjust Edits:** Drag the edit points in the Program Monitor to adjust the in and out points of the clip. Use the Trim Mode controls to view and edit the transitions between clips in detail.

- **Practical Applications:**
  - Ideal for making detailed adjustments to clip timing and ensuring seamless transitions between edits.

## 5. Keyboard Shortcuts for Trimming:

- **Ripple Trim Previous Edit to Playhead:**
  - **Shortcut:** Press "Q" to trim the beginning of a

clip to the playhead position.

- **Ripple Trim Next Edit to Playhead:**
  - ◦ **Shortcut:** Press "W" to trim the end of a clip to the playhead position.

- **Extend or Shorten Clip Duration:**
  - ◦ **Shortcut:** Hold down the Alt key (Option key on macOS) and drag the edge of a clip to extend or shorten its duration.

6. **Using the Trim Tool in the Timeline:**

- **Trim Tool:**
  - ◦ **Access:** Select the Trim Tool from the Tools panel or use keyboard shortcuts.
  - ◦ **Edge Trimming:** Click and drag the edge of a clip in the Timeline to adjust its in or out point. This technique is useful for quick adjustments directly within the Timeline view.

7. **Precise Timecode Adjustments:**

- **Input Timecode:**
  - ◦ **Direct Entry:** Right-click on the clip's edge and select "Timecode" to enter a specific timecode for precise trimming.

- **Review and Adjust:**
  - ◦ **Playback Review:** Use the Program Monitor to review the trimmed content and ensure accuracy before finalizing the edits.

By mastering these advanced trimming techniques, you can achieve greater precision and control over your video edits, ensuring that your content flows smoothly and effectively.

# MULTI-CAMERA EDITING

**M**ulti-camera editing is a powerful feature in Adobe Premiere Pro that allows you to seamlessly switch between multiple camera angles or shots during post-production. This is particularly useful for events, interviews, and any project where multiple perspectives are captured. Here's how to use multi-camera editing effectively:

1. **Setting Up Multi-Camera Editing:**

- **Prepare Your Clips:**
    - Ensure that all camera angles or takes are imported into the Project panel and are synchronized in terms of timecode or markers.

- **Create a Multi-Camera Sequence:**
    - **Select Clips:** Highlight the clips you want to include in the multi-camera sequence.
    - **Right-Click and Choose 'Create Multi-Camera Source Sequence':** This will open a dialog box.
    - **Sync Method:** Choose the sync method (e.g., Timecode, Audio, or In/Out Points). Timecode is the most precise if your cameras support it.

- ◦ **Click 'OK':** Premiere Pro will create a new sequence with all the selected clips synchronized and nested.

## 2. Editing with Multi-Camera Sequence:

- **Open the Multi-Camera Sequence:**
  - ◦ **Timeline View:** Open the newly created multi-camera sequence in the Timeline.
  - ◦ **Enable Multi-Camera View:** Click on the '+' button on the Program Monitor and drag the 'Multi-Camera' view option to the Program Monitor's toolbar.

- **Switching Angles:**
  - ◦ **Multi-Camera View:** In the Program Monitor, you will see the view of all camera angles.
  - ◦ **Live Switching:** Play the sequence and click on the camera angles in the Program Monitor to switch between them in real-time as the sequence plays.

- **Using Keyboard Shortcuts:**
  - ◦ **Angle Switching:** Use the number keys (1, 2, 3, etc.) to switch between camera angles during playback. Ensure that your multi-camera sequence is active and playing.

## 3. Fine-Tuning Multi-Camera Edits:

- **Adjusting Cuts:**
  - ◦ **Switch Angles:** While in the Timeline view, you can adjust the cuts by dragging the edges of the multi-camera clips to change which angles are shown at specific points.

- **Syncing Issues:**
  - ◦ **Re-sync Clips:** If there are syncing issues, you can manually adjust the synchronization by

dragging clips in the Timeline or using the 'Synchronize' feature.

- **Editing Angles:**
  - ◦ **Cutting and Adjusting:** You can cut and adjust clips in the multi-camera sequence just like a regular sequence. This allows for precise edits and adjustments to the angle switches.

## 4. Multi-Camera Editing Tips:

- **Organize Clips:**
  - ◦ **Label and Organize:** Label your camera angles and organize them into bins in the Project panel to keep track of different shots and perspectives.

- **Check Sync:**
  - ◦ **Verify Synchronization:** Before finalizing your edits, check that all angles are correctly synchronized and that there are no mismatches in the sequence.

- **Use Markers:**
  - ◦ **Add Markers:** Use markers in the Timeline to note key points where you want to switch camera angles. This can help streamline the editing process.

- **Practice Switching:**
  - ◦ **Playback Practice:** Practice switching between angles during playback to get a feel for how the transitions will look and feel in the final edit.

- **Review Final Edit:**
  - ◦ **Preview and Review:** Always review your final edit to ensure that the angle switches are smooth and that the overall flow of the video is cohesive.

By mastering multi-camera editing, you can enhance your video projects with dynamic camera angles and seamless transitions, resulting in a more engaging and professional final product.

# WORKING WITH SEQUENCES

Sequences in Adobe Premiere Pro are the foundation of your video project, where you arrange and edit your clips to create a final product. Understanding how to work with sequences efficiently is crucial for a smooth editing workflow. Here's a detailed guide:

1. **Creating a New Sequence:**

- **Using the New Sequence Dialog:**
    - **Create a Sequence:** Go to File > New > Sequence.
    - **Choose a Preset:** Select a preset that matches your project's settings (e.g., 1080p, 4K, frame rate). Presets are optimized for different camera formats and delivery requirements.
    - **Customize Settings:** If needed, adjust settings like frame rate, resolution, and audio sample rate in the New Sequence dialog.
    - **Click 'OK':** Premiere Pro will create a new sequence based on the selected preset and settings.

- **Drag and Drop Clips:**

- **Automatically Create Sequence:** Drag a clip from the Project panel to the Timeline. Premiere Pro will automatically create a new sequence that matches the clip's settings.

## 2. Managing Multiple Sequences:

- **Creating Additional Sequences:**
  - **Duplicate a Sequence:** Right-click on an existing sequence in the Project panel and choose 'Duplicate' to create a copy with the same settings.
  - **Create New:** Use the same steps as creating the first sequence to make additional sequences.

- **Switching Between Sequences:**
  - **Sequence Tabs:** Click on the tabs at the top of the Timeline panel to switch between open sequences.
  - **Open Sequence:** Double-click a sequence in the Project panel to open it in the Timeline.

- **Renaming Sequences:**
  - **Rename in Project Panel:** Right-click on the sequence name in the Project panel and choose 'Rename' to give it a descriptive name.

## 3. Working Within a Sequence:

- **Timeline Panel:**
  - **Navigating the Timeline:** Use scroll bars, the zoom slider, and the playhead to navigate through your sequence.
  - **Adjusting Tracks:** Add or remove video and audio tracks by right-clicking in the track header area and selecting 'Add Track' or 'Delete Track.'

- **Editing Clips in Sequence:**

- **Cutting and Trimming:** Use tools like the Razor Tool, Ripple Edit Tool, and Rolling Edit Tool to make precise cuts and adjustments.

- **Moving Clips:** Drag and drop clips to reposition them within the sequence.

- **Inserting and Overwriting:** Use the Insert and Overwrite functions to add new clips or replace existing ones.

## 4. Sequence Settings and Adjustments:

- **Modifying Sequence Settings:**
    - **Access Settings:** Go to Sequence > Sequence Settings to adjust settings such as frame size, pixel aspect ratio, and audio settings.
    - **Apply Changes:** Modify settings as needed and click 'OK' to apply changes.

- **Adjusting Sequence In/Out Points:**
    - **Set In/Out Points:** Use the Mark In (I) and Mark Out (O) buttons to define the start and end points of the sequence for playback or export.
    - **Adjust with Timeline Controls:** Drag the sequence's In and Out points in the Timeline to adjust the range.

## 5. Using Markers and Labels:

- **Adding Markers:**
    - **Set Markers:** Press "M" to add a marker at the playhead position. Right-click on the marker to rename or adjust its settings.
    - **Use for Notes:** Add markers to highlight important points or notes in your sequence.

- **Color Labels:**

- **Apply Labels:** Right-click on a clip and choose 'Label' to apply a color label. This helps in organizing and identifying clips easily.

## 6. Exporting a Sequence:

- **Export Settings:**
    - **Access Export Menu:** Go to File > Export > Media to open the Export Settings dialog.
    - **Choose Format:** Select the desired export format and preset based on your delivery requirements (e.g., H.264 for web, ProRes for high quality).
    - **Set Output Name and Location:** Choose a file name and destination for your exported video.

- **Exporting:**
    - **Export Process:** Click 'Export' or 'Queue' (to use Adobe Media Encoder) to begin the rendering and export process.

## 7. Sequence Tips and Best Practices:

- **Organize Your Timeline:**
    - **Use Track Headers:** Label and organize tracks for better management, such as separating video, audio, and effects tracks.

- **Maintain Sequence Backup:**
    - **Save Versions:** Keep backup copies of your sequences to safeguard against accidental changes or corruption.

- **Regularly Save Your Project:**
    - **Frequent Saves:** Save your project frequently to avoid losing changes and ensure that you have the most recent version.

By mastering these sequence management techniques, you can streamline your editing process and create more organized, efficient, and polished video projects.

# CHAPTER 4: AUDIO EDITING AND MIXING

# IMPORTING AND MANAGING AUDIO TRACKS

Proper management of audio tracks is crucial for achieving a professional sound in your video projects. This chapter covers how to import and manage audio tracks effectively in Adobe Premiere Pro.

1. **Importing Audio Tracks:**

- **Importing Audio Files:**
  - **Drag and Drop:** Drag audio files directly from your file explorer into the Project panel in Premiere Pro.

  - **File Menu:** Go to File > Import, navigate to your audio files, select them, and click 'Open.' The files will appear in the Project panel.

- **Using Media Browser:**
  - **Access Media Browser:** Open the Media Browser panel (Window > Media Browser).

  - **Navigate to Audio Files:** Browse to the folder containing your audio files.

  - **Import Files:** Right-click on the files and select

'Import' to add them to your Project panel.

- **Importing Audio from Video:**
  - **Extract Audio:** If your video clips contain embedded audio, Premiere Pro automatically imports the audio track. You can extract and manage it by dragging the video clip to the Timeline.

## 2. Managing Audio Tracks:

- **Organizing Audio in Project Panel:**
  - **Create Bins:** Organize audio files into bins within the Project panel for easy management. Right-click in the Project panel and choose 'New Bin' to create a new folder.
  - **Labeling:** Use color labels and rename audio files to identify them quickly.

- **Audio Track Layout:**
  - **Add Tracks:** Right-click on the track header area in the Timeline and choose 'Add Audio Track' to add more tracks as needed.
  - **Track Labels:** Rename audio tracks (e.g., Dialogue, Music, Sound Effects) for better organization.

- **Managing Track Volume:**
  - **Track Volume Control:** Use the volume sliders on the track header to adjust the overall volume of each audio track.
  - **Keyframe Adjustments:** Add keyframes to adjust volume levels at specific points by clicking the timeline and dragging the volume line up or down.

- **Track Mute and Solo:**
  - **Mute:** Click the 'Mute' button (speaker icon) on

a track to silence it during playback.

- **Solo:** Click the 'Solo' button to hear only the selected track while muting all other tracks.

- **Audio Clip Management:**
  - **Clip Adjustment:** Click and drag audio clips on the Timeline to reposition them. Trim audio clips by dragging the edges.
  - **Audio Fades:** Add fade-in or fade-out effects by dragging the fade handles at the beginning or end of the audio clip.

- **Audio Effects and Transitions:**
  - **Applying Effects:** Go to the Effects panel (Window > Effects) and drag audio effects (e.g., EQ, reverb) onto the audio clip in the Timeline.
  - **Audio Transitions:** Apply audio transitions (e.g., Constant Power) by dragging them from the Effects panel onto the edit points between audio clips.

- **Using the Essential Sound Panel:**
  - **Access Essential Sound Panel:** Go to Window > Essential Sound to open the panel.
  - **Audio Types:** Assign audio types (e.g., Dialogue, Music, Sound Effects) to clips for tailored editing and mixing options.
  - **Audio Processing:** Use the Essential Sound panel to quickly apply preset audio adjustments and enhancements.

3. **Audio Syncing:**

- **Synchronizing Audio and Video:**
  - **Sync by Timecode:** If your audio and video clips were recorded with matching timecodes, use the 'Synchronize' feature (right-click on

selected clips in the Timeline and choose 'Synchronize').

- **Manual Syncing:** Align audio manually by dragging clips in the Timeline to match the visual cues.

- **Adjusting Sync Issues:**
  - **Trim and Slide:** Use trimming and sliding techniques to correct any timing issues between audio and video.

## 4. Exporting Audio:

- **Audio Export Settings:**
  - **Export Audio Only:** Go to File > Export > Media. Choose an audio format (e.g., WAV, MP3) from the Format dropdown.

  - **Audio Export Options:** Adjust settings such as sample rate and bit depth as needed for your project.

- **Export Audio with Video:**
  - **Include Audio:** When exporting a video, ensure that audio tracks are included by selecting the appropriate settings in the Export Settings dialog.

## 5. Audio Editing Tips:

- **Use Headphones:** For accurate audio editing, use high-quality headphones or speakers.

- **Monitor Levels:** Regularly check audio levels to avoid distortion or clipping. Use the audio meters to monitor levels during playback.

- **Clean Up Audio:** Use noise reduction and audio repair tools to clean up background noise and enhance audio quality.

By following these steps, you can efficiently manage your audio tracks, ensuring clear and well-balanced sound in your video projects.

# BASIC AUDIO EDITING

asic audio editing in Adobe Premiere Pro involves
essential tasks such as cutting, trimming, adjusting
volume, and applying effects to improve the quality and
clarity of your audio. Here's how to handle these basic tasks:

1. **Cutting and Trimming Audio Clips:**

- **Cutting Audio Clips:**
  - **Select the Razor Tool:** Press "C" on your keyboard to activate the Razor Tool.

  - **Make Cuts:** Click on the audio clip in the Timeline where you want to make a cut. This splits the clip into segments.

  - **Switch to Selection Tool:** Press "V" to return to the Selection Tool. You can now move or delete the cut segments.

- **Trimming Audio Clips:**
  - **Drag Edges:** Position your cursor at the beginning or end of the audio clip until it turns into a trim handle. Drag to shorten or extend the clip.

  - **Adjust In/Out Points:** You can also trim audio by adjusting the In and Out points directly in the Timeline.

## 2. Adjusting Volume Levels:

- **Using the Volume Slider:**
  - ○ **Track Volume Control:** Locate the volume slider in the track header area of the Timeline. Adjust the volume level of the entire track by moving the slider up or down.

- **Adding Keyframes:**
  - ○ **Enable Keyframes:** Click on the "Show Keyframes" button in the Timeline (located in the track header) to display the volume line.
  - ○ **Add Keyframes:** Click on the volume line to create keyframes. Drag these keyframes to adjust the volume level at specific points in the clip.

- **Adjusting Clip Volume:**
  - ○ **Clip Adjustment:** Right-click on the audio clip and select 'Audio Gain.' Enter a specific gain level or adjust the gain by dragging the slider.

## 3. Applying Audio Effects:

- **Using the Effects Panel:**
  - ○ **Access Effects:** Go to Window > Effects to open the Effects panel.
  - ○ **Apply Effects:** Drag desired audio effects (e.g., EQ, Reverb) from the Effects panel onto the audio clip in the Timeline.

- **Adjusting Effects:**
  - ○ **Effect Controls Panel:** Select the audio clip and open the Effect Controls panel (Window > Effect Controls) to adjust the parameters of applied effects.
  - ○ **Customize Settings:** Tweak settings such as frequency, gain, and reverb amount to achieve

the desired sound.

## 4. Adding Fades and Transitions:

- **Applying Fades:**
    - **Fade In/Out:** Drag the fade handles (located at the beginning or end of an audio clip) to create fade-in or fade-out effects. The handles look like small circles or rectangles at the clip edges.
    - **Adjust Fade Duration:** Drag the handles further in or out to adjust the duration of the fade effect.

- **Audio Transitions:**
    - **Add Transitions:** Drag audio transitions (e.g., Constant Power) from the Effects panel to the edit points between audio clips to create smooth audio transitions.
    - **Adjust Transition Length:** Drag the edges of the transition effect in the Timeline to adjust its duration.

## 5. Using the Essential Sound Panel:

- **Access Essential Sound Panel:**
    - **Open Panel:** Go to Window > Essential Sound to open the Essential Sound panel.

- **Assign Audio Types:**
    - **Categorize Clips:** Select an audio clip in the Timeline and assign it an audio type (e.g., Dialogue, Music, Sound Effects) using the Essential Sound panel.
    - **Apply Presets:** Use the panel to apply preset adjustments to enhance audio quality, such as reducing background noise or improving clarity.

## 6. Monitoring and Adjusting Audio:

- **Use Audio Meters:**
  - **Monitor Levels:** Watch the audio meters (usually located at the top of the program window) to ensure audio levels are within the desired range and avoid distortion.

- **Check Audio Balance:**
  - **Balance Audio:** Adjust audio balance by panning audio clips left or right using the Pan control in the Effect Controls panel.

## 7. Previewing and Fine-Tuning:

- **Playback:** Regularly preview your audio edits by playing back the sequence to ensure that the edits sound natural and meet your expectations.

- **Make Adjustments:** Fine-tune volume levels, effects, and transitions based on playback to achieve the best audio quality.

By mastering these basic audio editing techniques, you can significantly enhance the sound quality and overall production value of your video projects.

# USING AUDIO EFFECTS AND FILTERS

Applying audio effects and filters in Adobe Premiere Pro can enhance your audio tracks, improve clarity, and create desired soundscapes. Here's how to use audio effects and filters effectively:

1. **Applying Audio Effects:**

- **Accessing Audio Effects:**
  - **Open the Effects Panel:** Go to Window > Effects to open the Effects panel.
  - **Locate Audio Effects:** In the Effects panel, expand the 'Audio Effects' folder to see a list of available audio effects.

- **Applying an Effect:**
  - **Drag and Drop:** Drag the desired audio effect from the Effects panel onto the audio clip in the Timeline.
  - **Apply to Track:** To apply an effect to an entire track, drag it onto the track's header or the track's audio clip.

- **Adjusting Effect Settings:**
  - **Effect Controls Panel:** With the audio clip

selected, go to Window > Effect Controls to open the Effect Controls panel.

- **Modify Parameters:** Adjust the effect parameters (e.g., Reverb amount, EQ frequencies) as needed.

2. **Using Common Audio Effects:**

- **Equalizer (EQ):**
  - **Purpose:** Adjusts the balance of different frequency ranges in your audio.
  - **Settings:** Use EQ effects like 'Parametric Equalizer' or 'Graphic Equalizer' to boost or cut specific frequency bands for clarity and balance.

- **Reverb:**
  - **Purpose:** Adds a sense of space or ambiance to your audio, simulating different environments.
  - **Settings:** Adjust parameters such as 'Decay Time,' 'Room Size,' and 'Wet/Dry Mix' to control the reverb effect.

- **Noise Reduction:**
  - **Purpose:** Reduces background noise or unwanted hum in your audio.
  - **Settings:** Use effects like 'DeNoiser' or 'Adaptive Noise Reduction' and adjust parameters to reduce noise while preserving audio quality.

- **Compression:**
  - **Purpose:** Controls the dynamic range of your audio by reducing the volume of loud sounds and boosting quieter sounds.
  - **Settings:** Adjust 'Threshold,' 'Ratio,' 'Attack,'

and 'Release' to manage compression levels and maintain audio consistency.

- **Echo:**
  - ○ **Purpose:** Adds an echo effect to create a sense of space or enhance vocal presence.
  - ○ **Settings:** Modify parameters like 'Delay Time,' 'Feedback,' and 'Wet/Dry Mix' to achieve the desired echo effect.

## 3. Using Audio Filters:

- **Accessing Filters:**
  - ○ **Open the Effects Panel:** Go to Window > Effects.
  - ○ **Locate Audio Filters:** Expand the 'Audio Filters' folder to find available filters.

- **Applying a Filter:**
  - ○ **Drag and Drop:** Drag the desired audio filter onto the audio clip in the Timeline.
  - ○ **Track Application:** To apply a filter to an entire track, drag it onto the track's header.

- **Adjusting Filter Settings:**
  - ○ **Effect Controls Panel:** With the audio clip selected, open the Effect Controls panel.
  - ○ **Modify Parameters:** Adjust the filter settings (e.g., 'High Pass,' 'Low Pass') to tailor the audio effect to your needs.

## 4. Creating Custom Audio Presets:

- **Save Custom Presets:**
  - ○ **Adjust Effects:** After configuring an effect to your liking, click the 'Effect Controls' panel menu (three horizontal lines) and choose 'Save Preset.'

- **Name and Save:** Give your preset a name and save it for future use.

- **Apply Presets:**
  - **Access Presets:** Use the 'Presets' folder in the Effects panel to find and apply your saved custom presets to new audio clips.

## 5. Fine-Tuning and Monitoring:

- **Preview Changes:**
  - **Playback:** Regularly play back your audio to hear the effects in context and make necessary adjustments.

- **Monitor Levels:**
  - **Check Meters:** Use audio meters to ensure that effects are not causing distortion or clipping.

- **Adjust Effect Intensity:**
  - **Effect Amount:** Fine-tune the amount of effect applied using the parameters in the Effect Controls panel to balance the effect with the original audio.

## 6. Removing and Resetting Effects:

- **Removing Effects:**
  - **Select and Delete:** In the Effect Controls panel, select the effect you want to remove and click the trash can icon or right-click and choose 'Remove.'

- **Resetting Effects:**
  - **Reset Settings:** In the Effect Controls panel, right-click the effect and choose 'Reset' to return it to its default settings.

By mastering these audio effects and filters, you can enhance your audio tracks, address issues, and create a polished sound for your video projects.

# MIXING AND BALANCING AUDIO

**M**ixing and balancing audio is crucial for achieving a professional and cohesive sound in your video projects. This process involves adjusting the levels, panning, and effects of different audio tracks to ensure clarity and balance. Here's a guide to help you mix and balance audio effectively in Adobe Premiere Pro:

1. **Understanding Audio Tracks:**

- **Types of Tracks:**
  - **Dialogue:** Typically consists of spoken content that should be clear and prominent.
  - **Music:** Provides background or mood and should complement the dialogue without overpowering it.
  - **Sound Effects:** Includes ambient sounds or specific audio cues, which should be balanced to enhance the video without being intrusive.

2. **Setting Up for Mixing:**

- **Organize Your Tracks:**
  - **Label Tracks:** Rename tracks in the Timeline (e.g., Dialogue, Music, SFX) for easy

identification.

- **Group Related Clips:** Use bins and labels in the Project panel to group and organize audio clips by type.

- **Use the Audio Mixer Panel:**
  - **Open Mixer:** Go to Window > Audio Track Mixer to access the Audio Mixer panel.
  - **Track Controls:** The Audio Mixer allows you to control each track's volume, pan, and apply effects.

## 3. Adjusting Volume Levels:

- **Set Initial Levels:**
  - **Use Volume Sliders:** In the Audio Mixer panel, adjust the volume sliders for each track to set initial levels.
  - **Balance Dialogue:** Ensure dialogue is at a clear and understandable level, typically the most prominent in the mix.

- **Fine-Tune Levels:**
  - **Monitor Meters:** Use audio meters to ensure levels are within the desired range. Avoid clipping (peaking into the red zone).
  - **Adjust Keyframes:** Use volume keyframes in the Timeline to adjust levels at specific points, such as lowering music during dialogue.

## 4. Panning Audio:

- **Stereo Panning:**
  - **Pan Controls:** In the Audio Mixer panel, use the pan knobs to position audio in the stereo field (left, center, right).
  - **Create Depth:** Pan different elements to create

a sense of space and depth in your audio mix.

- **Balancing Tracks:**
  - ◦ **Balance Position:** Ensure that no single track dominates the mix unless intentionally desired (e.g., a solo vocal).

## 5. Applying Audio Effects:

- **Use Effects Sparingly:**
  - ◦ **Add Effects:** Apply effects such as EQ, compression, and reverb to individual tracks or the entire mix as needed.
  - ◦ **Avoid Overprocessing:** Apply effects in moderation to avoid making the audio sound unnatural or cluttered.

- **Adjust Effect Parameters:**
  - ◦ **Effect Controls:** Fine-tune effect settings using the Effect Controls panel to achieve the desired sound without overwhelming the mix.

## 6. Creating and Using Audio Submixes:

- **Add Submixes:**
  - ◦ **Create Submixes:** In the Audio Track Mixer, add submixes to group and control multiple tracks together.
  - ◦ **Route Tracks:** Route audio tracks to the submix for combined control over groups of tracks (e.g., all music tracks).

- **Adjust Submix Levels:**
  - ◦ **Mix Submixes:** Adjust the volume and effects of submixes to balance their overall contribution to the final mix.

## 7. Monitoring and Final Adjustments:

- **Use Headphones or Studio Monitors:**

- ○ **Monitor Sound:** Use high-quality headphones or studio monitors to accurately hear the mix and make precise adjustments.

- **Check in Different Environments:**
  - ○ **Playback on Various Devices:** Test the final mix on different playback systems (e.g., speakers, headphones, TV) to ensure it sounds good across various devices.

- **Final Tweaks:**
  - ○ **Adjust Levels:** Make final adjustments to volume, panning, and effects based on playback results and feedback.

## 8. Exporting the Final Mix:

- **Export Audio Mix:**
  - ○ **Go to Export:** Go to File > Export > Media.
  - ○ **Choose Format:** Select the desired format (e.g., WAV, MP3) and adjust export settings for audio quality.
  - ○ **Export Settings:** Ensure audio export settings match your project requirements (e.g., bit rate, sample rate).

By mastering these mixing and balancing techniques, you can ensure that all audio elements in your video project are clear, well-integrated, and professionally presented.

# CHAPTER 5: ADDING AND CUSTOMIZING EFFECTS

# APPLYING VIDEO EFFECTS

Applying video effects in Adobe Premiere Pro can enhance the visual appeal of your projects, add stylistic elements, and correct or improve footage. This section covers the fundamental processes for applying and customizing video effects.

1. **Accessing Video Effects:**

- **Open the Effects Panel:**
  - **Navigate to Effects:** Go to Window > Effects to open the Effects panel.
  - **Locate Video Effects:** Expand the 'Video Effects' folder to access the list of available effects.

2. **Applying a Video Effect:**

- **Drag and Drop:**
  - **Select Effect:** Choose the desired effect from the Effects panel.
  - **Apply to Clip:** Drag the effect onto the video clip in the Timeline where you want to apply it.

- **Applying to Multiple Clips:**

- **Batch Apply:** Select multiple clips in the Timeline, then drag and drop the effect onto any of the selected clips to apply it to all selected clips.

3. **Customizing Video Effects:**

- **Effect Controls Panel:**
    - **Open Effect Controls:** Select the video clip with the effect applied, then go to Window > Effect Controls to open the Effect Controls panel.
    - **Adjust Effect Parameters:** Modify the effect's settings, such as intensity, color, and position, using the sliders and controls in the Effect Controls panel.

- **Keyframing Effects:**
    - **Enable Keyframes:** Click the stopwatch icon next to the effect parameter you want to animate to enable keyframing.
    - **Add Keyframes:** Move the playhead to different points in the Timeline and adjust the parameter values to create keyframes for animation.
    - **Adjust Keyframes:** Drag keyframes in the Timeline to adjust the timing and smoothness of the effect transitions.

4. **Using Preset Effects:**

- **Access Presets:**
    - **Find Presets:** In the Effects panel, expand the 'Presets' folder to find predefined effect settings.
    - **Apply Preset:** Drag a preset onto a video clip to apply a combination of effects with pre-

configured settings.

- **Create and Save Custom Presets:**
  - ◦ **Customize Effects:** Adjust effect parameters to your desired settings.
  - ◦ **Save Preset:** In the Effect Controls panel, click the Effects panel menu (three horizontal lines) and choose 'Save Preset.' Name and save your custom preset for future use.

## 5. Effect Blending and Opacity:

- **Adjust Blending Modes:**
  - ◦ **Select Blending Mode:** In the Effect Controls panel, use the 'Opacity' section to change the blending mode of the effect (e.g., Multiply, Screen).
  - ◦ **Blend Effects:** Experiment with blending modes to combine effects in different ways and achieve unique looks.

- **Adjust Opacity:**
  - ◦ **Change Opacity:** Use the opacity slider in the Effect Controls panel to adjust the transparency of the effect.
  - ◦ **Animate Opacity:** Add keyframes to animate opacity changes over time.

## 6. Applying Color Correction and Grading Effects:

- **Color Correction Effects:**
  - ◦ **Apply Effects:** Use effects like 'Lumetri Color,' 'Three-Way Color Corrector,' and 'Fast Color Corrector' to adjust exposure, contrast, and color balance.
  - ◦ **Adjust Settings:** Modify settings to correct color issues and enhance the visual quality of your footage.

- **Color Grading Effects:**
  - **Create Look:** Use effects like 'Lumetri Color' to apply creative color grading for a specific look or mood.
  - **Use LUTs:** Apply Lookup Tables (LUTs) for predefined color grading styles and easily achieve professional looks.

## 7. Animating Effects:

- **Position and Scale Animation:**
  - **Keyframe Animation:** Use keyframes to animate position, scale, and rotation of effects over time.
  - **Effect Controls Panel:** Adjust position, scale, and rotation parameters and add keyframes to animate these properties.

- **Masking and Tracking Effects:**
  - **Create Masks:** Use the masking tools in the Effect Controls panel to create and animate masks for selective effect application.
  - **Track Motion:** Apply tracking to masks and effects to follow moving objects within the video.

## 8. Previewing and Fine-Tuning Effects:

- **Playback:** Regularly preview your video with effects applied to check how they interact with the footage.
- **Fine-Tuning:** Make adjustments to effect parameters and keyframes as needed based on playback results.

## 9. Removing and Resetting Effects:

- **Remove Effects:**
  - **Select and Delete:** In the Effect Controls panel, select the effect you want to remove and click

the trash can icon or right-click and choose 'Remove.'

- **Reset Effects:**
  - **Reset Settings:** In the Effect Controls panel, right-click the effect and choose 'Reset' to return it to default settings.

By understanding how to apply and customize video effects, you can enhance your video projects with professional-quality visuals and achieve the desired aesthetic or corrective results.

# CUSTOMIZING EFFECTS AND PRESETS

Customizing effects and presets in Adobe Premiere Pro allows you to tailor effects to fit your specific needs and create a unique look for your projects. Here's a detailed guide on how to customize video effects and create your own presets:

1. **Customizing Individual Effects:**

- **Access Effect Controls:**
    - **Select Clip:** Click on the video clip in the Timeline to which the effect is applied.
    - **Open Effect Controls:** Go to Window > Effect Controls to view and adjust the effect settings.

- **Adjust Effect Parameters:**
    - **Modify Settings:** Use the sliders, color pickers, and other controls in the Effect Controls panel to adjust the effect's parameters (e.g., intensity, color balance, blur amount).
    - **Preview Changes:** Adjust settings while previewing the video to see the effect in real-

time and fine-tune as needed.

- **Use Keyframes for Animation:**
  - **Enable Keyframing:** Click the stopwatch icon next to a parameter to enable keyframes.
  - **Add Keyframes:** Move the playhead to different points in the Timeline and adjust the parameter to create keyframes that animate the effect over time.
  - **Adjust Keyframes:** Drag keyframes in the Timeline to refine the timing and smoothness of the animation.

2. **Creating and Saving Custom Presets:**

- **Customize Effects:**
  - **Apply and Adjust Effects:** Apply the desired effects to a clip and adjust their settings to achieve your desired look.

- **Save Preset:**
  - **Open Effect Controls:** With the clip selected, go to the Effect Controls panel.
  - **Save Preset:** Click on the Effects panel menu (three horizontal lines) and choose 'Save Preset.'
  - **Name and Description:** Enter a name and optional description for your preset. Choose from options like 'Scale' (for effects relative to clip size) or 'Anchor to In Point' (for effects starting at the clip's in point).
  - **Save Preset:** Click 'OK' to save the custom preset for future use.

- **Applying Custom Presets:**
  - **Locate Presets:** In the Effects panel, expand the 'Presets' folder to find your saved presets.

- ◦ **Apply Preset:** Drag the preset onto a new clip or existing clips to apply the customized effect settings.

## 3. Creating Presets with Multiple Effects:

- **Combine Effects:**
  - ◦ **Apply Multiple Effects:** Add and adjust multiple effects to a clip as needed.
  - ◦ **Save as Preset:** Follow the same steps to save the combination of effects as a single preset.

- **Organize Presets:**
  - ◦ **Use Bins:** Create bins in the Project panel to organize and categorize your custom presets for easier access.

## 4. Managing and Editing Presets:

- **Editing Presets:**
  - ◦ **Apply and Modify:** Apply a saved preset to a clip, then make adjustments in the Effect Controls panel as needed.
  - ◦ **Save Updated Preset:** Save the updated settings as a new preset or overwrite the existing one.

- **Deleting Presets:**
  - ◦ **Remove Preset:** In the Effects panel, right-click the preset you want to delete and choose 'Delete.'

## 5. Creating Presets for Specific Scenarios:

- **Special Effects:**
  - ◦ **Design Custom Looks:** Create presets for specific scenarios, such as a particular color grading style or a unique transition effect.

- **Efficient Workflow:**

- ○ **Save Time:** Use custom presets to quickly apply consistent effects across multiple clips or projects.

## 6. Using Third-Party Presets:

- • **Import Presets:**
  - ○ **Install Presets:** Import third-party presets by dragging them into the Effects panel or using File > Import.
  - ○ **Apply and Customize:** Apply imported presets and adjust settings to fit your project needs.

By mastering the customization of effects and presets, you can streamline your workflow, maintain consistency across projects, and achieve a polished and professional look for your videos.

# USING KEYFRAMES FOR ANIMATION

**K**eyframes in Adobe Premiere Pro are essential for animating effects, properties, and transitions over time. They allow you to create dynamic changes and effects by defining specific points of change and controlling the animation between them. Here's a comprehensive guide to using keyframes for animation:

1. **Understanding Keyframes:**

- **Definition:** Keyframes mark specific points in time where you define a value for an effect or property. Premiere Pro automatically interpolates the values between keyframes to create smooth animations.

- **Types of Keyframes:**
    - **Linear Keyframes:** Create a constant rate of change between keyframes.
    - **Bezier Keyframes:** Allow for custom speed and easing adjustments between keyframes.

2. **Applying Keyframes:**

- **Open Effect Controls:**
    - **Select Clip:** Click on the video clip in the Timeline that you want to animate.

- **Effect Controls:** Go to Window > Effect Controls to open the Effect Controls panel.

- **Enable Keyframing:**
  - **Select Property:** Find the property or effect you want to animate (e.g., Position, Scale, Opacity).
  - **Activate Keyframing:** Click the stopwatch icon next to the property to enable keyframes. A keyframe is automatically added at the current playhead position.

3. **Adding and Adjusting Keyframes:**

- **Add Keyframes:**
  - **Move Playhead:** Position the playhead where you want to add a new keyframe.
  - **Adjust Value:** Change the property value (e.g., move the position, scale the image).
  - **Add Keyframe:** A new keyframe will be added automatically when you adjust the property.

- **Adjust Keyframe Values:**
  - **Select Keyframe:** Click on a keyframe in the Timeline or Effect Controls panel.
  - **Modify Value:** Adjust the value of the property to change the keyframe's effect.

4. **Editing Keyframes:**

- **Move Keyframes:**
  - **Drag Keyframes:** Click and drag keyframes in the Effect Controls panel or Timeline to change their position and timing.

- **Delete Keyframes:**
  - **Select and Delete:** Click on a keyframe and press Delete, or right-click and choose 'Clear'

to remove it.

- **Change Keyframe Interpolation:**
    - **Right-Click Keyframe:** Right-click on a keyframe in the Effect Controls panel or Timeline.
    - **Choose Interpolation:** Select 'Linear,' 'Bezier,' or 'Hold' to adjust how the animation transitions between keyframes.

## 5. Using Bezier Keyframes:

- **Add Bezier Keyframes:**
    - **Select Keyframe:** Right-click a keyframe and choose 'Temporal Interpolation' > 'Bezier' for a smooth, customizable transition.

- **Adjust Bezier Handles:**
    - **Edit Handles:** Use the handles on the keyframe in the Effect Controls panel to adjust the speed and curve of the animation.

## 6. Animating Multiple Properties:

- **Apply Keyframes to Different Properties:**
    - **Keyframe Multiple Properties:** Add keyframes for different properties (e.g., Position, Scale, Opacity) to create complex animations involving multiple effects.

- **Synchronize Animations:**
    - **Align Keyframes:** Align keyframes across different properties to synchronize animations and ensure smooth transitions.

## 7. Using Keyframes with Effects:

- **Animate Effect Parameters:**
    - **Apply Effect:** Add an effect (e.g., Blur, Color Correction) to a clip.

- ◦ **Animate Parameters:** Use keyframes to animate the effect's parameters (e.g., gradually increase blur over time).

## 8. Previewing and Fine-Tuning:

- **Preview Animation:**
  - ◦ **Playhead:** Use the playhead to preview the animation and ensure it looks as expected.
  - ◦ **Adjust Keyframes:** Make necessary adjustments to keyframes based on the preview.

- **Smooth Animation:**
  - ◦ **Refine Interpolation:** Use Bezier handles and adjust keyframe interpolation to create smooth and natural animations.

## 9. Copying and Pasting Keyframes:

- **Copy Keyframes:**
  - ◦ **Select and Copy:** Select keyframes in the Effect Controls panel or Timeline, then use Edit > Copy.

- **Paste Keyframes:**
  - ◦ **Position Playhead:** Move the playhead to the desired location.
  - ◦ **Paste:** Use Edit > Paste to apply the copied keyframes to the new location.

## 10. Animating with Presets:

- **Apply Animation Presets:**
  - ◦ **Find Presets:** In the Effects panel, explore animation presets for common effects and transitions.
  - ◦ **Apply and Adjust:** Drag and drop presets onto your clip, then adjust keyframes as needed to

fit your project.

By effectively using keyframes, you can create dynamic and engaging animations, transitions, and effects in your video projects, adding a professional touch and enhancing the viewer's experience.

# CREATING AND USING LUTS (LOOK-UP TABLES)

LUTs (Look-Up Tables) are powerful tools in color grading and correction that help achieve consistent and professional looks in your video projects. They map one color space to another, allowing for quick and precise color adjustments. Here's a guide to creating and using LUTs in Adobe Premiere Pro:

1. **Understanding LUTs:**

- **Definition:** A LUT is a mathematical formula that adjusts colors in your footage based on a predefined set of values. LUTs can be used to apply color grading, correct color imbalances, or achieve specific looks.

- **Types of LUTs:**
    - **Technical LUTs:** Used for color correction and balancing.
    - **Creative LUTs:** Used for stylistic color grading and achieving specific looks.

2. **Applying LUTs:**

- **Using Built-In LUTs:**
  - **Open Lumetri Color Panel:** Go to Window > Lumetri Color to open the Lumetri Color panel.
  - **Select LUT:** In the Lumetri Color panel, go to the 'Basic Correction' section. Click the 'Input LUT' dropdown menu to select a built-in LUT from the available options.
  - **Apply LUT:** Choose the desired LUT to apply it to your footage.

- **Using Custom LUTs:**
  - **Import Custom LUTs:** Click the 'Browse' button next to the 'Input LUT' dropdown menu in the Lumetri Color panel to import a custom LUT file (.cube or .look).
  - **Select and Apply:** Navigate to the location of your custom LUT file, select it, and apply it to your footage.

3. **Creating Custom LUTs:**

- **Color Grading in Premiere Pro:**
  - **Apply Base Adjustments:** Use the Lumetri Color panel to adjust color settings, including Basic Correction, Creative, Curves, Color Wheels, and HSL Secondary.
  - **Fine-Tune Look:** Make detailed color adjustments and grading to achieve your desired look.

- **Export LUT:**
  - **Open Lumetri Color Panel:** Once you have your look finalized, open the Lumetri Color panel.
  - **Save LUT:** Go to the Lumetri Color panel menu (three horizontal lines) and select

'Export .cube.' Choose a location to save your custom LUT file.

## 4. Using LUTs in Your Projects:

- **Apply LUTs to Multiple Clips:**
  - ○ **Copy and Paste:** Apply a LUT to one clip, then copy the Lumetri Color effect and paste it onto other clips to maintain a consistent look.
  - ○ **Adjustment Layers:** Apply a LUT to an adjustment layer above multiple clips in the Timeline to apply the same look to all clips.

- **Adjusting LUT Intensity:**
  - ○ **Modify Intensity:** In the Lumetri Color panel, adjust the 'Intensity' or 'Amount' slider under the 'Basic Correction' section to control the strength of the applied LUT.
  - ○ **Blend with Other Effects:** Combine LUTs with other color correction effects to achieve a balanced look.

## 5. Managing LUTs:

- **Organize LUTs:**
  - ○ **Create Folders:** Organize LUTs into folders in your 'Creative' or 'Technical' LUT directories for easy access.

- **Backup and Share:**
  - ○ **Save and Backup:** Keep backup copies of your custom LUTs and share them with others if needed.

## 6. Troubleshooting LUTs:

- **Check Compatibility:** Ensure that the LUT file format (.cube, .look) is supported by Premiere Pro.

- **Adjust Settings:** If the LUT doesn't look as expected,

tweak the settings in the Lumetri Color panel or make adjustments to the footage before applying the LUT.

7. **Tips for Effective LUT Use:**

- **Use LUTs as a Starting Point:** Apply LUTs as a base for your color grading, and make further adjustments to fine-tune the look.

- **Monitor Consistency:** Ensure that the LUT applied maintains consistency across different shots and scenes in your project.

- **Test on Different Monitors:** View your footage on various monitors to ensure that the LUT's look is consistent across different display devices.

By effectively creating and using LUTs, you can streamline your color grading workflow, achieve consistent and professional results, and enhance the overall visual impact of your video projects.

# CHAPTER 6: COLOR CORRECTION AND GRADING

# UNDERSTANDING COLOR CORRECTION BASICS

Color correction and grading are fundamental processes in video editing that ensure your footage looks visually appealing and consistent. Color correction addresses issues in color balance and exposure, while color grading adds stylistic elements to achieve a specific look or mood. This section covers the basics of color correction and grading in Adobe Premiere Pro.

1. **Color Correction Fundamentals:**

- **Purpose:**
    - **Correct Color Issues:** Address and fix color imbalances, exposure problems, and white balance issues in your footage.

    - **Ensure Consistency:** Achieve uniformity in color and exposure across different shots and scenes.

- **Basic Color Correction Tools:**
    - **Lumetri Color Panel:** Provides a comprehensive set of tools for color correction and grading. Accessible via Window > Lumetri

Color.

- ◦ **Scopes:** Monitor color and exposure levels using scopes such as the Vectorscope, Histogram, and Waveform Monitor.

## 2. Adjusting White Balance:

- **White Balance Controls:**
  - ◦ **Lumetri Color Panel:** In the 'Basic Correction' section, use the 'White Balance' controls to adjust the temperature and tint of your footage.
  - ◦ **Temperature:** Adjusts the overall warmth or coolness of the image.
  - ◦ **Tint:** Corrects color casts by adjusting green and magenta hues.

- **Using White Balance Selector:**
  - ◦ **Select Neutral Area:** Use the White Balance Selector tool in the Lumetri Color panel to click on a neutral gray or white area in your footage.
  - ◦ **Automatic Adjustment:** Premiere Pro will automatically adjust the white balance based on the selected area.

## 3. Correcting Exposure and Contrast:

- **Exposure Adjustment:**
  - ◦ **Lumetri Color Panel:** In the 'Basic Correction' section, adjust the 'Exposure' slider to correct the overall brightness of the footage.
  - ◦ **Highlight and Shadow Controls:** Fine-tune the exposure by adjusting highlights and shadows to recover details in bright and dark areas.

- **Contrast Adjustment:**

- **Contrast Slider:** Adjust the 'Contrast' slider to increase or decrease the difference between the light and dark areas of your footage.

## 4. Adjusting Color Levels:

- **RGB Color Wheels:**
  - **Lumetri Color Panel:** Use the 'Color Wheels' section to adjust midtones, shadows, and highlights separately for more precise color correction.

- **Curves:**
  - **RGB Curves:** Use the 'Curves' section to adjust the overall brightness and contrast by manipulating the RGB curves. The curve can be adjusted to correct color balance and achieve specific looks.

## 5. Using Color Scopes:

- **Vectorscope:**
  - **Analyze Color Balance:** Use the Vectorscope to monitor color balance and saturation. It displays the color distribution of your footage.

- **Histogram:**
  - **Monitor Exposure:** Use the Histogram to check exposure levels and ensure that highlights and shadows are within the desired range.

- **Waveform Monitor:**
  - **Analyze Luminance:** Use the Waveform Monitor to measure the luminance levels across the image. It helps in adjusting exposure and ensuring proper contrast.

## 6. Creating a Balanced Look:

- **Match Shots:**

- **Ensure Consistency:** Use the Lumetri Color panel to match color and exposure between different shots for a cohesive look throughout the project.

- **Copy and Paste Settings:** Copy color correction settings from one clip and paste them onto other clips to maintain consistency.

- **Check for Overexposure and Underexposure:**
  - **Monitor Scopes:** Regularly check the scopes to ensure that there are no clipped highlights or crushed shadows in your footage.

## 7. Basic Color Grading:

- **Creative Looks:**
  - **Apply LUTs:** Use Look-Up Tables (LUTs) to apply creative color grading presets and achieve specific looks or moods.

  - **Adjust LUT Intensity:** Control the intensity of LUTs to fine-tune the applied look.

- **Creative Adjustments:**
  - **Use Color Wheels:** Adjust color balance and add stylistic color grading using the color wheels in the Lumetri Color panel.

  - **Apply Filters:** Use additional effects and filters to enhance the overall look and feel of your footage.

## 8. Previewing and Fine-Tuning:

- **Preview Corrections:**
  - **Playback:** Regularly preview your footage to check the impact of color corrections and grading.

  - **Make Adjustments:** Fine-tune corrections and grading based on the preview results.

- **Consistent Monitoring:**
  - **Use Reference Monitors:** View your footage on a calibrated reference monitor to ensure accurate color representation.

By understanding the basics of color correction and grading, you can enhance the visual quality of your footage, achieve a consistent look across your project, and add stylistic elements to make your videos more engaging and professional.

# USING THE LUMETRI COLOR PANEL

The Lumetri Color panel in Adobe Premiere Pro is a comprehensive tool for color correction and grading. It allows you to make precise adjustments to color balance, exposure, and creative looks. Here's how to effectively use the Lumetri Color panel:

1. **Opening the Lumetri Color Panel:**

   - **Access Panel:**
     - **Navigate to Window:** Go to Window > Lumetri Color to open the Lumetri Color panel.
     - **Panel Layout:** The panel typically appears on the right side of the workspace.

2. **Basic Correction:**

   - **White Balance:**
     - **Adjust Temperature:** Use the 'Temperature' slider to make your footage warmer or cooler.
     - **Adjust Tint:** Use the 'Tint' slider to correct green or magenta color casts.
     - **Auto White Balance:** Click the White Balance Selector tool and select a neutral gray or white area in the footage to automatically adjust the

white balance.

- **Exposure and Contrast:**
    - **Exposure:** Adjust the 'Exposure' slider to correct the overall brightness.
    - **Contrast:** Increase or decrease the 'Contrast' slider to enhance or reduce the difference between light and dark areas.
    - **Highlights and Shadows:** Adjust the 'Highlights' and 'Shadows' sliders to recover details in bright and dark areas.
- **Whites and Blacks:**
    - **Whites:** Adjust the 'Whites' slider to control the brightest parts of the image.
    - **Blacks:** Adjust the 'Blacks' slider to control the darkest parts of the image.

3. **Creative Adjustments:**

- **Creative Looks:**
    - **Apply LUTs:** In the 'Creative' section, click the 'Input LUT' dropdown to apply a built-in or custom LUT (Look-Up Table).
    - **Adjust LUT Intensity:** Use the 'Intensity' slider to control how strongly the LUT affects your footage.
    - **Faded Film and Vignette:** Adjust the 'Faded Film' and 'Vignette' sliders to add stylistic effects.
- **Color Wheels:**
    - **Shadows, Midtones, and Highlights:** Use the 'Color Wheels' section to adjust the color balance in shadows, midtones, and highlights independently.

- **Adjust Color Balance:** Drag the color wheel to adjust the color and intensity of each tonal range.

4. **Curves:**

- **RGB Curves:**
  - **Adjust Brightness and Contrast:** Use the 'RGB Curves' section to adjust the overall brightness and contrast by manipulating the curve.
  - **Individual Color Channels:** Adjust the Red, Green, and Blue channels separately for precise color grading.

- **Hue vs. Saturation and Hue vs. Hue Curves:**
  - **Hue vs. Saturation:** Modify the saturation of specific color ranges using the 'Hue vs. Saturation' curve.
  - **Hue vs. Hue:** Adjust the hue of specific color ranges using the 'Hue vs. Hue' curve.

5. **HSL Secondary:**

- **Isolate Colors:**
  - **Color Range:** Use the 'HSL Secondary' section to isolate and adjust specific colors in your footage.
  - **Adjust HSL Controls:** Modify 'Hue,' 'Saturation,' and 'Lightness' for the selected color range.
  - **Refine Selection:** Use the 'Add Color Mask' or 'Refine' controls to fine-tune the color selection.

6. **Vignette:**

- **Apply Vignette:**
  - **Amount:** Adjust the 'Amount' slider to control

the strength of the vignette effect.

- **Midpoint, Roundness, and Feather:** Adjust the 'Midpoint,' 'Roundness,' and 'Feather' sliders to customize the vignette's appearance and softness.

7. **Using Keyframes:**

- **Animate Adjustments:**
    - **Enable Keyframes:** Click the stopwatch icon next to any parameter (e.g., Exposure, Saturation) to enable keyframes for animation.
    - **Add Keyframes:** Move the playhead to different points in the Timeline and adjust the parameter to create keyframes that animate the effect over time.

8. **Copying and Pasting Color Settings:**

- **Copy Settings:**
    - **Select Clip:** Click on the clip with the desired color settings.
    - **Copy Effects:** Right-click and select 'Copy' or use Ctrl+C (Cmd+C on Mac) to copy the Lumetri Color settings.

- **Paste Settings:**
    - **Select Target Clip:** Click on the clip where you want to apply the color settings.
    - **Paste Effects:** Right-click and select 'Paste' or use Ctrl+V (Cmd+V on Mac) to apply the copied settings.

9. **Preview and Fine-Tuning:**

- **View Changes:**
    - **Playback:** Regularly play back your footage

to view the impact of color adjustments and grading.

- **Adjust as Needed:** Make further adjustments based on the preview to refine the look.

## 10. Saving and Using Presets:

- **Save Presets:**
  - **Save Settings:** Once you've achieved a desired look, go to the Lumetri Color panel menu (three horizontal lines) and select 'Save Preset' to save your settings as a custom preset.

- **Apply Presets:**
  - **Load Presets:** Drag and drop saved presets from the 'Effects' panel onto your clips or adjustment layers to apply consistent color settings.

By effectively using the Lumetri Color panel, you can achieve precise color correction, enhance your footage with creative grading, and maintain consistency throughout your video projects.

# COLOR GRADING TECHNIQUES

Color grading enhances the mood, style, and visual impact of your footage. Here's a comprehensive guide to color grading techniques using Adobe Premiere Pro:

1. **Basic Color Grading Workflow:**

   - **Start with Color Correction:**
     - ◦ **Correct Exposure and White Balance:** Use the Lumetri Color panel's 'Basic Correction' section to fix exposure, contrast, and white balance issues before applying creative grading.

   - **Apply a Base Look:**
     - ◦ **Use LUTs:** Apply a Look-Up Table (LUT) for a starting point and adjust its intensity to achieve a foundational look.

2. **Creative Color Grading:**

   - **Use Color Wheels:**
     - ◦ **Shadows, Midtones, and Highlights:** Adjust the color balance for shadows, midtones, and highlights using the 'Color Wheels' section in the Lumetri Color panel.

     - ◦ **Create Mood:** Shift colors to create specific

moods or styles (e.g., warm tones for a nostalgic feel, cool tones for a modern look).

- **Apply Curves:**
  - ○ **RGB Curves:** Adjust the RGB curves to manipulate the overall brightness and contrast. Create S-curves for enhanced contrast or smooth curves for softer looks.
  - ○ **Hue Curves:** Use the 'Hue vs. Saturation' and 'Hue vs. Hue' curves to adjust specific color ranges and achieve more nuanced color grading.

## 3. Color Effects and Adjustments:

- **Adjust Saturation and Vibrance:**
  - ○ **Saturation:** Increase or decrease overall saturation to intensify or mute colors.
  - ○ **Vibrance:** Adjust vibrance to enhance the saturation of less intense colors while preserving skin tones and other critical colors.

- **Use HSL Secondary:**
  - ○ **Isolate Colors:** Use the HSL Secondary section to isolate and adjust specific colors or color ranges.
  - ○ **Refine Color Mask:** Modify the hue, saturation, and lightness of isolated colors to fine-tune their appearance.

## 4. Creating and Applying Presets:

- **Save Custom Looks:**
  - ○ **Create Presets:** After achieving a desired look, save your settings as a preset for reuse. Go to the Lumetri Color panel menu and select 'Save Preset.'

- **Apply Presets:**

- **Load Presets:** Drag and drop saved presets onto clips or adjustment layers to apply consistent color grading across multiple clips.

## 5. Vignette and Special Effects:

- **Apply Vignette:**
  - **Add Vignette:** In the Lumetri Color panel, use the 'Vignette' section to add a vignette effect. Adjust the 'Amount,' 'Midpoint,' 'Roundness,' and 'Feather' settings to create a subtle darkening around the edges.

- **Apply Special Effects:**
  - **Creative Filters:** Experiment with creative filters and effects to add stylistic elements to your footage, such as grain, blur, or glow.

## 6. Matching Color Across Clips:

- **Match Shots:**
  - **Use Comparison View:** Use the 'Comparison View' tool in the Lumetri Color panel to compare color grading between different clips and ensure consistency.

  - **Adjust Color:** Fine-tune the color grading settings to match shots and scenes for a cohesive look.

## 7. Using Adjustment Layers:

- **Apply Global Changes:**
  - **Create Adjustment Layer:** Add an adjustment layer above your clips in the Timeline to apply color grading effects globally.

  - **Adjust Color:** Use the Lumetri Color panel on the adjustment layer to affect all underlying clips with consistent grading.

## 8. Previewing and Fine-Tuning:

- **Regular Previewing:**
  - **Playback:** Continuously play back your footage to review the impact of color grading adjustments.
  - **Make Adjustments:** Refine settings based on playback to ensure the color grading enhances the footage as intended.

## 9. Color Grading for Different Media:

- **For Different Formats:**
  - **Consider Medium:** Adjust your color grading technique based on the medium (e.g., web, television, film) to ensure optimal appearance on various display devices.

## 10. Exporting and Sharing:

- **Export Settings:**
  - **Check Final Look:** Ensure that your color grading looks consistent in the exported version of your video.
  - **Monitor Calibration:** Export and view the video on different monitors to confirm color accuracy and consistency.

By mastering these color grading techniques, you can elevate the visual quality of your footage, create engaging and stylistic looks, and ensure a professional finish to your video projects.

# MATCHING COLOR ACROSS CLIPS

E nsuring color consistency across different clips is crucial for a cohesive visual style in your project. Adobe Premiere Pro offers several tools and techniques to match color effectively. Here's a step-by-step guide to help you achieve consistent color grading:

1. **Using the Comparison View Tool:**

- **Open Comparison View:**
  - **Navigate to the Lumetri Color Panel:** Go to Window > Lumetri Color to open the panel.
  - **Enable Comparison View:** Click on the 'Comparison View' button in the Lumetri Color panel (it looks like two side-by-side images).

- **Select Comparison Clips:**
  - **Choose Reference Clip:** Select a reference clip from the 'Reference Monitor' section. This will be your target look.
  - **Compare with Current Clip:** Compare the color grading of the current clip with the reference clip to ensure consistency.

2. **Using Color Match in Lumetri Color Panel:**

- **Open Color Match Tool:**
  - **Select Clip:** Choose the clip you want to match.
  - **Navigate to Lumetri Color Panel:** In the Lumetri Color panel, go to the 'Color Wheels & Match' section.

- **Apply Color Match:**
  - **Select Reference:** Click on the 'Apply Match' button in the 'Color Wheels & Match' section to use the color match tool.
  - **Adjust Match Settings:** The tool will automatically adjust the color of your clip to match the reference clip. Fine-tune adjustments as needed.

3. **Manual Color Matching:**

- **Use Color Wheels:**
  - **Adjust Shadows, Midtones, and Highlights:** In the Lumetri Color panel, use the 'Color Wheels' section to manually adjust the color balance in shadows, midtones, and highlights to match the reference clip.

- **Adjust Curves:**
  - **RGB Curves:** Use the 'RGB Curves' section to adjust the overall brightness and contrast. Modify the curves to match the color and tonal range of the reference clip.

- **Fine-Tune with HSL Secondary:**
  - **Isolate Colors:** Use the 'HSL Secondary' section to isolate and adjust specific color ranges. Match these adjustments with the reference clip to achieve consistency.

4. **Copying and Pasting Color Settings:**

- **Copy Settings:**
  - **Select Correct Clip:** Apply the desired color grading settings to a reference clip.
  - **Copy Effects:** Right-click the clip and select 'Copy' or use Ctrl+C (Cmd+C on Mac) to copy the Lumetri Color settings.

- **Paste Settings:**
  - **Select Target Clips:** Click on the clips where you want to apply the color settings.
  - **Paste Effects:** Right-click and select 'Paste' or use Ctrl+V (Cmd+V on Mac) to apply the copied settings to the target clips.

5. **Using Adjustment Layers:**

- **Create Adjustment Layer:**
  - **Add to Timeline:** Add an adjustment layer above your clips in the Timeline by going to File > New > Adjustment Layer.
  - **Apply Color Grading:** Apply color grading effects to the adjustment layer to uniformly apply the same look across multiple clips.

6. **Checking Consistency Across Devices:**

- **Monitor Calibration:**
  - **Check on Different Screens:** View your project on different monitors or devices to ensure that the color grading appears consistent across various displays.

7. **Using Scopes for Accuracy:**

- **Vectorscope:**
  - **Analyze Color Balance:** Use the Vectorscope to monitor color balance and ensure consistency in color saturation and hue.

- **Histogram:**
  - ◦ **Monitor Exposure Levels:** Use the Histogram to check exposure levels and make sure that highlights and shadows are consistent.

- **Waveform Monitor:**
  - ◦ **Analyze Luminance:** Use the Waveform Monitor to measure luminance levels and ensure proper contrast and brightness across clips.

By using these techniques and tools, you can achieve consistent and professional color grading across your project, ensuring a cohesive visual style and enhancing the overall quality of your video.

# CHAPTER 7: TITLES AND GRAPHICS

# CREATING AND EDITING TITLES

**T**itles and graphics add essential visual elements to your video, helping to convey information, create emphasis, and enhance the overall look. Adobe Premiere Pro offers robust tools for creating and editing titles. Here's a detailed guide on how to effectively create and manage titles and graphics in Premiere Pro:

1. **Creating Basic Titles:**

- **Open the Essential Graphics Panel:**
  - **Navigate to Window:** Go to Window > Essential Graphics to open the Essential Graphics panel.

- **Create a New Title:**
  - **Click on New Layer:** In the Essential Graphics panel, click on the 'New Layer' button and select 'Text' to create a new text layer.

- **Add and Customize Text:**
  - **Type Your Text:** Click on the Program Monitor and start typing your text. You can enter titles, subtitles, or any text elements.

  - **Customize Font and Style:** Use the 'Edit' tab

in the Essential Graphics panel to adjust the font, size, color, and style. You can also use the character and paragraph formatting options.

## 2. Using Title Templates:

- **Browse Templates:**
    - ◦ **Browse Available Templates:** In the Essential Graphics panel, use the 'Browse' tab to explore and select pre-designed title templates.
    - ◦ **Drag and Drop Template:** Drag a template from the panel to the Timeline to use it in your project.

- **Customize Templates:**
    - ◦ **Edit Text and Style:** Double-click on the template in the Timeline to open it in the Essential Graphics panel. Customize the text, colors, and other design elements as needed.

## 3. Positioning and Animating Titles:

- **Position and Align:**
    - ◦ **Move Text:** Use the Selection Tool (V) to drag and position your text on the Program Monitor.
    - ◦ **Align Text:** Use alignment tools in the Essential Graphics panel to center or position text relative to the screen or other elements.

- **Animate Titles:**
    - ◦ **Add Keyframes:** Select the text layer in the Timeline, then use the Effect Controls panel to add keyframes for position, scale, and opacity to create animations.
    - ◦ **Use Presets:** Apply animation presets from the Effects panel to quickly add motion to your titles.

## 4. Creating Graphics and Lower Thirds:

- **Add Graphics:**
  - **New Layer:** In the Essential Graphics panel, click on 'New Layer' and select 'Shape' or 'Image' to add graphical elements.
  - **Design Graphics:** Use the 'Edit' tab to customize shapes, colors, and sizes. Add logos, icons, or other graphic elements as needed.

- **Design Lower Thirds:**
  - **Create Lower Thirds:** Use text and shape layers to design lower thirds that appear at the bottom of the screen. Position and style them according to your project's needs.

## 5. Working with Motion Graphics Templates (MOGRTs):

- **Import MOGRTs:**
  - **Download or Create MOGRTs:** Download motion graphics templates (MOGRTs) from Adobe Stock or create your own in Adobe After Effects.
  - **Import into Premiere Pro:** Use the Essential Graphics panel to import and use MOGRTs in your project.

- **Customize MOGRTs:**
  - **Edit Templates:** Select the MOGRT in the Essential Graphics panel and adjust text, colors, and other settings based on your project requirements.

## 6. Editing and Managing Titles and Graphics:

- **Edit Text and Graphics:**
  - **Select Layer:** Click on the text or graphic layer in the Timeline to select it.
  - **Make Changes:** Use the Essential Graphics

panel to edit text content, fonts, colors, and graphic properties.

- **Manage Layers:**
    - ◦ **Organize Layers:** Use the Layers panel to arrange and organize multiple text and graphic layers. Adjust layer order and visibility as needed.

- **Apply Effects:**
    - ◦ **Add Effects:** Use the Effects panel to apply additional effects such as drop shadows, glows, or transitions to enhance your titles and graphics.

## 7. Previewing and Fine-Tuning:

- **Preview Changes:**
    - ◦ **Playback:** Regularly play back your project to view how titles and graphics look in context.
    - ◦ **Adjust as Needed:** Make further adjustments to text, positioning, and animations based on the preview.

- **Check for Consistency:**
    - ◦ **Review All Titles:** Ensure consistency in style and positioning across all titles and graphics in your project.

## 8. Exporting Titles and Graphics:

- **Render Titles:**
    - ◦ **Final Export:** Ensure titles and graphics are properly rendered in the final export of your project. Check for clarity and readability in different video formats and resolutions.

By mastering these techniques, you can create professional and engaging titles and graphics that enhance the overall quality of your video projects.

# USING GRAPHICS AND TEMPLATES

Adobe Premiere Pro provides powerful tools for incorporating graphics and templates into your video projects. These elements can enhance the visual appeal of your content and streamline your editing workflow. Here's how to effectively use graphics and templates:

1. **Using Essential Graphics Panel:**

- **Open the Essential Graphics Panel:**
  - **Access Panel:** Go to Window > Essential Graphics to open the panel, where you can create and manage graphics and text elements.

- **Browse and Search for Templates:**
  - **Explore Templates:** In the Essential Graphics panel, switch to the 'Browse' tab to view available motion graphics templates (MOGRTs) and title templates.
  - **Search Templates:** Use the search bar to find specific templates based on keywords or categories.

2. **Adding and Customizing Graphics:**

- **Add Graphics to Your Timeline:**

- **Drag and Drop:** Drag a graphic or template from the Essential Graphics panel onto your Timeline where you want it to appear in your video.

- **Customize Text and Styles:**
  - **Edit Text:** Click on the graphic or text layer in the Program Monitor to edit the text content. Use the Essential Graphics panel to change font, size, color, and other text properties.
  - **Adjust Style:** Modify styles such as text alignment, spacing, and shadow effects to match your project's design.

- **Customize Graphics:**
  - **Edit Shapes and Colors:** Use the 'Edit' tab in the Essential Graphics panel to change the shapes, colors, and sizes of graphic elements. Adjust graphical properties to fit your project's aesthetic.

3. **Creating and Using Motion Graphics Templates (MOGRTs):**

- **Import MOGRTs:**
  - **Access Templates:** Click on the 'Browse' tab in the Essential Graphics panel and select 'Browse Adobe Stock' or 'Import Motion Graphics Template' to add MOGRTs to your project.

- **Apply and Customize MOGRTs:**
  - **Drag to Timeline:** Drag a MOGRT from the Essential Graphics panel to the Timeline.
  - **Edit MOGRTs:** Select the MOGRT in the Timeline, then use the Essential Graphics panel to customize text, colors, and other properties.

### 4. Creating Your Own Graphics:

- **Add New Graphics:**
  - ○ **New Layer:** In the Essential Graphics panel, click 'New Layer' and choose from options like 'Text,' 'Shape,' or 'Image' to create custom graphics.
  - ○ **Design Graphics:** Use the 'Edit' tab to design and style your graphics. You can add text, shapes, and images as needed.

- **Save Custom Templates:**
  - ○ **Create Template:** After designing a graphic, save it as a template for future use. In the Essential Graphics panel, click on the 'Export As Motion Graphics Template' button to save your custom design.

### 5. Animating Graphics:

- **Add Keyframes:**
  - ○ **Select Layer:** Click on the graphic or text layer in the Timeline.
  - ○ **Open Effect Controls:** Use the Effect Controls panel to add keyframes for position, scale, opacity, and other properties to create animations.

- **Apply Animation Presets:**
  - ○ **Browse Presets:** In the Effects panel, find animation presets under 'Motion' or 'Effects.'
  - ○ **Drag and Drop:** Apply animation presets by dragging them onto your graphic or text layer.

### 6. Managing and Organizing Graphics:

- **Layer Management:**
  - ○ **Organize Layers:** Use the Layers panel to manage multiple graphics and text layers.

Adjust layer order and visibility to ensure proper stacking and visibility in your project.

- **Group and Align:**
  - **Group Elements:** Group related graphic elements together to manage them more easily.
  - **Align and Distribute:** Use alignment tools to position graphics precisely within the Program Monitor.

## 7. Previewing and Fine-Tuning:

- **Playback:**
  - **Review Graphics:** Regularly play back your video to check how graphics and templates look in context.
  - **Make Adjustments:** Adjust settings and positioning based on playback to ensure that graphics enhance the video effectively.

## 8. Exporting and Sharing Graphics:

- **Render Graphics:**
  - **Check Quality:** Ensure that graphics and templates are rendered clearly in the final export. Check for readability and visual consistency across different video formats.

By mastering these techniques, you can effectively use graphics and templates to enhance your video projects, create engaging visual elements, and streamline your editing workflow.

# ANIMATING TEXT AND GRAPHICS

Animating text and graphics adds dynamic elements to your video, making it more engaging and visually appealing. Adobe Premiere Pro offers several tools and techniques to animate these elements effectively. Here's a detailed guide to animating text and graphics:

**1. Basic Animation with Keyframes:**

- **Select the Layer:**
  - **Choose Layer:** Click on the text or graphic layer in the Timeline that you want to animate.

- **Open Effect Controls:**
  - **Navigate to Effect Controls:** Go to Window > Effect Controls to open the panel where you can adjust animation properties.

- **Add Keyframes:**
  - **Position Keyframes:** Click the stopwatch icon next to properties like Position, Scale, Rotation, or Opacity to add keyframes. Keyframes mark the start and end points of your animation.

- **Adjust Keyframes:** Move the playhead in the Timeline and adjust the property values to set different positions, sizes, or effects at different times.

## 2. Animating Text:

- **Text Animation Presets:**
  - **Browse Presets:** In the Effects panel, look under the 'Effects' tab for text animation presets like 'Animate In' and 'Animate Out.'
  - **Apply Presets:** Drag and drop a preset onto your text layer to apply pre-defined animations.

- **Customize Text Animation:**
  - **Adjust Preset Settings:** After applying a preset, go to the Effect Controls panel to customize animation settings such as duration, easing, and direction.

## 3. Animating Graphics:

- **Shape and Image Animation:**
  - **Apply Keyframes:** Use keyframes to animate properties such as Position, Scale, and Rotation for shapes and images.
  - **Create Motion Paths:** Adjust Position keyframes to create motion paths or movements for graphical elements.

- **Use the Transform Effect:**
  - **Apply Transform Effect:** In the Effects panel, search for and apply the 'Transform' effect to your graphic layer for advanced animation options.
  - **Animate Transform Properties:** Use the Transform effect to animate properties like

Position, Scale, and Rotation with more control.

## 4. Animating with Presets and Effects:

- **Apply Animation Presets:**
  - ○ **Browse Presets:** In the Effects panel, find animation presets under categories like 'Motion' or 'Effects.'
  - ○ **Drag and Drop:** Apply the preset to your text or graphic layer and adjust settings in the Effect Controls panel.

- **Use Effects for Animation:**
  - ○ **Apply Effects:** Drag effects such as 'Blur,' 'Glow,' or 'Color Correction' onto your layer. Animate the effect properties using keyframes.

## 5. Using Adjustment Layers for Animation:

- **Create Adjustment Layer:**
  - ○ **Add Adjustment Layer:** Go to File > New > Adjustment Layer and add it above your text or graphic layers in the Timeline.
  - ○ **Animate on Adjustment Layer:** Apply and animate effects on the adjustment layer to affect multiple layers simultaneously.

## 6. Creating Complex Animations:

- **Use the Essential Graphics Panel:**
  - ○ **Animate MOGRTs:** Customize and animate Motion Graphics Templates (MOGRTs) using the Essential Graphics panel.
  - ○ **Edit Animation:** Open the MOGRT in the Essential Graphics panel and adjust animation settings or add keyframes.

- **Combine Multiple Animations:**
  - ◦ **Layer Animations:** Combine different animations for text and graphics by layering multiple effects and keyframes.
  - ◦ **Synchronize Animations:** Ensure that animations are synchronized and flow smoothly across your video.

## 7. Applying Easing for Smooth Transitions:

- **Add Easing:**
  - ◦ **Apply Easing:** Right-click on keyframes in the Timeline and choose easing options like 'Ease In,' 'Ease Out,' or 'Ease In/Out' for smoother transitions.
  - ◦ **Adjust Speed:** Use the Graph Editor in the Effect Controls panel to fine-tune the speed and acceleration of your animations.

## 8. Previewing and Fine-Tuning Animations:

- **Playback:**
  - ◦ **Check Animations:** Regularly play back your video to see how the animations look in context.
  - ◦ **Refine Adjustments:** Make adjustments to keyframes and settings based on playback to achieve the desired effect.

## 9. Exporting Animated Text and Graphics:

- **Render and Export:**
  - ◦ **Check Quality:** Ensure that animations are smooth and clear in the final export. Verify that text and graphics are rendered correctly in different resolutions and formats.

By mastering these animation techniques, you can create engaging and professional text and graphic animations that enhance the visual impact of your video projects.

# INTEGRATING WITH ADOBE AFTER EFFECTS

I ntegrating Adobe Premiere Pro with Adobe After Effects allows you to leverage the advanced motion graphics and visual effects capabilities of After Effects within your Premiere Pro projects. Here's how to effectively integrate these two powerful tools:

1. **Dynamic Link Overview:**

- **What is Dynamic Link?**
    - ◦ **Seamless Integration:** Dynamic Link is a feature that allows you to create a workflow between Premiere Pro and After Effects without rendering intermediate files.
    - ◦ **Real-Time Updates:** Changes made in After Effects are automatically updated in Premiere Pro, providing a smooth editing experience.

2. **Using Dynamic Link:**

- **Send Clips to After Effects:**
    - ◦ **Select Clip:** In Premiere Pro, select the clip or sequence you want to animate or add effects

to.

- **Right-Click and Choose 'Replace With After Effects Composition':** This will create a new composition in After Effects with the selected clip.

- **Edit in After Effects:** Make your changes in After Effects. You can use all the advanced tools and effects available.

- **Return to Premiere Pro:**
  - **Automatic Updates:** Once you save your After Effects project, the changes will automatically update in Premiere Pro. You don't need to manually import or render the updated file.

## 3. Creating and Importing After Effects Compositions:

- **Create a New Composition in After Effects:**
  - **Open After Effects:** Start by creating a new composition in After Effects with the settings matching your Premiere Pro project.

  - **Design and Animate:** Use After Effects to design and animate text, graphics, and effects.

- **Import into Premiere Pro:**
  - **Use Dynamic Link:** Go back to Premiere Pro and select File > Adobe Dynamic Link > Import After Effects Composition. Choose the After Effects project and composition to import.

  - **Use in Timeline:** The imported composition will appear in your Premiere Pro project panel. Drag it onto the timeline where needed.

## 4. Editing Dynamic Link Compositions:

- **Modify in After Effects:**
  - **Access Composition:** Double-click on the Dynamic Link composition in Premiere Pro to

open it in After Effects.

- **Make Adjustments:** Edit the composition as needed in After Effects. Changes will be reflected in Premiere Pro automatically.

## 5. Handling Complex Projects:

- **Organize Your Workflow:**
  - **Use Precomps:** In After Effects, use precompositions to organize complex animations and effects. This can help manage large projects more effectively.
  - **Layer Management:** Keep your layers organized and labeled to make editing easier.

- **Optimize Performance:**
  - **Use Proxies:** For complex effects, consider using proxies to speed up playback and editing in Premiere Pro.
  - **Manage Memory:** Ensure both Premiere Pro and After Effects have sufficient memory allocated to handle dynamic linking efficiently.

## 6. Rendering and Exporting:

- **Render Compositions:**
  - **Render in After Effects:** If you need to export a final version of the composition, render it directly in After Effects using the Render Queue or Adobe Media Encoder.
  - **Export Settings:** Choose appropriate export settings based on your project requirements and desired output format.

- **Final Export in Premiere Pro:**
  - **Export Project:** Once your project is complete in Premiere Pro, use the Export function (File >

Export > Media) to render the final video.

## 7. Troubleshooting Common Issues:

- **Check for Missing Files:**
    - ○ **File Paths:** Ensure that all file paths are correct and that no files are missing or relocated.

- **Resolve Playback Issues:**
    - ○ **Performance:** If playback is slow or choppy, adjust playback settings or use proxies in Premiere Pro.

- **Update Software:**
    - ○ **Compatibility:** Ensure both Adobe Premiere Pro and After Effects are updated to the latest versions to avoid compatibility issues.

By integrating Adobe After Effects with Premiere Pro, you can enhance your video projects with sophisticated animations and visual effects, making your workflow more efficient and your final product more polished.

# CHAPTER 8: EXPORTING AND RENDERING

# UNDERSTANDING EXPORT SETTINGS

Exporting and rendering are crucial final steps in the video production process, ensuring that your project is output in the correct format and quality for its intended use. Adobe Premiere Pro provides a variety of export settings to match different needs, from online sharing to high-quality archival. Here's a comprehensive guide to understanding and using export settings effectively:

1. **Overview of Export Formats:**

- **Common Formats:**
  - **H.264:** Ideal for web videos and social media. It offers a good balance between quality and file size. Export as MP4.

  - **QuickTime (MOV):** Suitable for high-quality video exports with a variety of codecs, often used for professional work.

  - **ProRes:** Offers high-quality video for editing and archival purposes. Larger file sizes but better quality retention.

  - **AVI:** A versatile format, though less common for web use due to large file sizes.

- **Resolution and Aspect Ratio:**
  - **Resolution:** Choose the resolution based on your project's needs, such as 1080p (Full HD) or 4K (Ultra HD).
  - **Aspect Ratio:** Ensure the aspect ratio matches your intended display, such as 16:9 for widescreen or 9:16 for vertical videos.

2. **Using the Export Media Dialog Box:**

- **Accessing Export Settings:**
  - **Open Export Dialog:** Go to File > Export > Media to open the Export Settings dialog box.

- **Export Presets:**
  - **Choose a Preset:** Adobe Premiere Pro offers several built-in presets for various platforms like YouTube, Vimeo, and Instagram. Select a preset that matches your export needs.
  - **Custom Settings:** For more control, you can customize settings beyond the presets.

3. **Adjusting Export Settings:**

- **Format:**
  - **Select Format:** Choose the format that best suits your needs (e.g., H.264 for web use, ProRes for high-quality output).

- **Preset:**
  - **Pick a Preset:** Select a preset that aligns with your export requirements. Customize settings if needed.

- **Output Name and Location:**
  - **Specify File Name:** Click on the output name to rename your file and choose the export location.

- **Video Settings:**
  - **Resolution:** Set the resolution to match your project (e.g., 1920x1080 for Full HD).
  - **Frame Rate:** Ensure the frame rate matches your project settings (e.g., 24fps, 30fps).
  - **Bitrate Settings:** Adjust bitrate to balance quality and file size. Higher bitrates offer better quality but result in larger files.

- **Audio Settings:**
  - **Audio Codec:** Choose an audio codec such as AAC for H.264 exports.
  - **Sample Rate and Bitrate:** Adjust sample rate (e.g., 48 kHz) and audio bitrate (e.g., 192 kbps) based on your quality requirements.

## 4. Using the Effects Panel:

- **Render Effects:**
  - **Render Settings:** Ensure that effects and adjustments made in Premiere Pro are rendered correctly. Check the 'Use Maximum Render Quality' box for better results.

- **Preview and Adjustments:**
  - **Preview Export:** Use the 'Source' and 'Output' tabs to preview your export settings and make any necessary adjustments.

## 5. Exporting with Media Encoder:

- **Queue to Media Encoder:**
  - **Send to Media Encoder:** Click on the 'Queue' button to send your project to Adobe Media Encoder for export.
  - **Batch Export:** Use Media Encoder to export multiple projects or sequences in batch, optimizing export time and workflow.

## 6. Optimizing Export Quality and File Size:

- **Balancing Quality and File Size:**
    - ◦ **Adjust Bitrate:** Lower bitrates reduce file size but may impact quality. Find a balance that suits your needs.
    - ◦ **Resolution Scaling:** If file size is a concern, consider scaling down the resolution.
- **Render at Maximum Depth:**
    - ◦ **Ensure Quality:** Check the 'Render at Maximum Depth' option for better color depth and detail.

## 7. Finalizing the Export:

- **Export and Review:**
    - ◦ **Start Export:** Click 'Export' or 'Queue' to begin the export process.
    - ◦ **Review Output:** Once the export is complete, review the final output to ensure it meets your quality and format requirements.

## 8. Troubleshooting Export Issues:

- **Check Export Errors:**
    - ◦ **Error Messages:** If you encounter errors, review error messages and ensure all settings are correctly configured.
    - ◦ **Re-export if Necessary:** Make adjustments to settings if the final output doesn't meet expectations.

By understanding and correctly configuring export settings, you can ensure that your video projects are rendered in the highest quality and suitable format for your intended audience or platform.

# EXPORTING
# FOR DIFFERENT
# PLATFORMS

**E**xporting video content for various platforms requires tailoring settings to meet the specific requirements and best practices of each platform. Here's a guide to exporting for popular platforms:

1. **YouTube:**

- **Format and Codec:**
    - **Format:** H.264
    - **Codec:** MP4 (preferred)
- **Resolution and Frame Rate:**
    - **Resolution:** 1920x1080 (Full HD) or 3840x2160 (4K)
    - **Frame Rate:** 24, 30, or 60 fps (depending on your source footage)
- **Bitrate Settings:**
    - **Bitrate:** For 1080p, use 8-12 Mbps; for 4K, use 35-45 Mbps.
- **Audio Settings:**

- **Codec:** AAC
- **Sample Rate:** 48 kHz
- **Bitrate:** 192 kbps or higher

- **Other Considerations:**
  - **File Size:** Ensure file size meets YouTube's upload limits.
  - **Aspect Ratio:** Maintain a 16:9 aspect ratio for standard widescreen.

2. **Vimeo:**

- **Format and Codec:**
  - **Format:** H.264
  - **Codec:** MP4 (preferred)

- **Resolution and Frame Rate:**
  - **Resolution:** 1920x1080 (Full HD) or 3840x2160 (4K)
  - **Frame Rate:** 24, 25, 30, 48, 50, or 60 fps

- **Bitrate Settings:**
  - **Bitrate:** For 1080p, use 8-12 Mbps; for 4K, use 20-30 Mbps.

- **Audio Settings:**
  - **Codec:** AAC
  - **Sample Rate:** 48 kHz
  - **Bitrate:** 192 kbps or higher

- **Other Considerations:**
  - **File Size:** Vimeo has a maximum file size limit for different account types.
  - **Aspect Ratio:** Maintain a 16:9 aspect ratio for standard widescreen.

3. **Instagram:**

- **Format and Codec:**
  - **Format:** MP4
  - **Codec:** H.264

- **Resolution and Frame Rate:**
  - **Resolution:** 1080x1080 (square) or 1080x1920 (vertical)
  - **Frame Rate:** 30 fps

- **Bitrate Settings:**
  - **Bitrate:** 3-5 Mbps

- **Audio Settings:**
  - **Codec:** AAC
  - **Sample Rate:** 44.1 kHz
  - **Bitrate:** 128 kbps

- **Other Considerations:**
  - **Aspect Ratio:** Use 1:1 for square videos, 4:5 for portrait, and 16:9 for landscape.
  - **Video Length:** Instagram limits video length to 60 seconds for regular posts and up to 15 minutes for IGTV.

## 4. Facebook:

- **Format and Codec:**
  - **Format:** MP4
  - **Codec:** H.264

- **Resolution and Frame Rate:**
  - **Resolution:** 1280x720 (HD) or 1920x1080 (Full HD)
  - **Frame Rate:** 30 fps

- **Bitrate Settings:**
  - **Bitrate:** 4-6 Mbps for HD

- **Audio Settings:**
  - **Codec:** AAC
  - **Sample Rate:** 44.1 kHz
  - **Bitrate:** 128 kbps

- **Other Considerations:**
  - **Aspect Ratio:** Use 16:9 for landscape and 4:5 for portrait.
  - **File Size:** Facebook supports large files but aim for optimization to reduce upload times.

5. **TikTok:**

- **Format and Codec:**
  - **Format:** MP4
  - **Codec:** H.264

- **Resolution and Frame Rate:**
  - **Resolution:** 1080x1920 (vertical)
  - **Frame Rate:** 30 fps

- **Bitrate Settings:**
  - **Bitrate:** 5-10 Mbps

- **Audio Settings:**
  - **Codec:** AAC
  - **Sample Rate:** 44.1 kHz
  - **Bitrate:** 128 kbps

- **Other Considerations:**
  - **Aspect Ratio:** Use 9:16 for full-screen vertical videos.
  - **Video Length:** TikTok supports videos up to 10 minutes.

6. **Websites and Blogs:**

- **Format and Codec:**

- **Format:** MP4
- **Codec:** H.264

- **Resolution and Frame Rate:**
  - **Resolution:** 1280x720 (HD) or 1920x1080 (Full HD)
  - **Frame Rate:** 24 or 30 fps

- **Bitrate Settings:**
  - **Bitrate:** 4-8 Mbps for HD

- **Audio Settings:**
  - **Codec:** AAC
  - **Sample Rate:** 44.1 kHz
  - **Bitrate:** 128 kbps

- **Other Considerations:**
  - **Aspect Ratio:** 16:9 is standard for most web content.
  - **Compression:** Use moderate compression to ensure good quality while keeping file sizes manageable.

By understanding the specific requirements of each platform and configuring your export settings accordingly, you can ensure optimal playback quality and compatibility for your video content.

# RENDERING OPTIONS AND BEST PRACTICES

Rendering is the final step in video production where your project is processed into a playable format. Choosing the right rendering options and following best practices can significantly impact the quality and efficiency of your export. Here's a comprehensive guide to rendering options and best practices:

1. **Rendering Options:**

- **Export Settings:**
  - **Format:** Choose the format based on your output needs (e.g., H.264 for web, ProRes for high-quality).
  - **Preset:** Use presets tailored for specific platforms or purposes (e.g., YouTube 1080p, Vimeo 4K).

- **Bitrate Settings:**
  - **Constant Bitrate (CBR):** Maintains a consistent bitrate throughout the video. Suitable for high-quality outputs.
  - **Variable Bitrate (VBR):** Adjusts the bitrate based on complexity. VBR 2-pass provides better quality by analyzing the video twice.

- **Resolution and Frame Rate:**
  - **Match Source:** For best results, match the export resolution and frame rate with your source footage.
  - **Scaling:** If scaling, ensure the aspect ratio is preserved to avoid distortion.
- **Render at Maximum Depth:**
  - **Enable Option:** Check 'Render at Maximum Depth' for better color accuracy and detail.
- **Use Maximum Render Quality:**
  - **Enable Option:** This setting improves the scaling quality and is recommended for high-quality exports.

## 2. Best Practices for Rendering:

- **Pre-Export Checks:**
  - **Review Project:** Ensure all edits, effects, and transitions are final.
  - **Check Audio Levels:** Verify that audio levels are balanced and not clipping.
- **Use Proxies for Editing:**
  - **Proxies:** Use lower-resolution proxies for smoother editing and switch to full-resolution files for final rendering.
- **Optimize Render Settings:**
  - **Bitrate and Quality:** Balance bitrate and quality based on the intended use (e.g., high bitrate for professional projects, lower bitrate for web use).
  - **Format Choice:** Choose formats and codecs that match your distribution platform requirements.

- **Hardware and Software Optimization:**
  - **Update Software:** Ensure Adobe Premiere Pro and related software are up to date.
  - **Optimize System:** Close unnecessary applications and ensure sufficient RAM and processing power.

- **Render in Sections if Needed:**
  - **Large Projects:** For very large projects, consider rendering in sections to manage file size and rendering time.

- **Use Adobe Media Encoder for Batch Processing:**
  - **Queue Multiple Exports:** Adobe Media Encoder allows you to queue multiple projects or sequences, optimizing export efficiency.

- **Monitor Output Quality:**
  - **Review Export:** Check the final export for quality, including color accuracy, audio synchronization, and overall playback.

- **Backup and Archive:**
  - **Save Backups:** Keep backups of your project files and final exports in case of future revisions or issues.
  - **Archive Projects:** Archive completed projects for future reference or potential re-use.

- **Test Different Settings:**
  - **Trial Exports:** Perform trial exports with different settings to find the best balance between quality and file size for your needs.

- **Stay Informed About Platform Requirements:**
  - **Platform Specifications:** Keep up to date with the latest specifications and recommendations for platforms where your

content will be distributed.

By following these rendering options and best practices, you can ensure that your video exports are of high quality, efficiently processed, and well-suited for their intended distribution platform.

# MANAGING OUTPUT FILES

E ffectively managing output files is crucial for ensuring smooth workflow, maintaining quality, and organizing your projects. Here's how to manage your output files efficiently:

1. **Organizing Output Files:**

  - **Create a Folder Structure:**
    - ◦ **Organize by Project:** Use a clear and consistent folder structure for each project (e.g., ProjectName/Exports/).
    - ◦ **Subfolders:** Create subfolders for different versions, formats, or deliverables (e.g., 1080p, 4K, Web, Archive).

  - **Naming Conventions:**
    - ◦ **Descriptive Names:** Use descriptive names for your files to easily identify their content and purpose (e.g., ProjectName_Version1_1080p.mp4).
    - ◦ **Version Control:** Include version numbers or dates to track different iterations (e.g., ProjectName_Final_v1.mp4).

## 2. Backing Up Output Files:

- **Regular Backups:**
    - **Use Backup Solutions:** Implement regular backups using external drives, cloud storage, or network-attached storage (NAS).
    - **Automated Backup:** Consider automated backup solutions to ensure files are regularly backed up.

- **Redundancy:**
    - **Multiple Locations:** Store backups in multiple locations to protect against data loss (e.g., local drive, cloud storage, external drives).

## 3. Archiving Projects:

- **Archive Completed Projects:**
    - **Organize Archives:** Store archived projects in a dedicated folder or drive (e.g., Archive/ProjectName/).
    - **Compression:** Compress large projects into zip files to save space (e.g., ProjectName_Archive.zip).

- **Metadata and Documentation:**
    - **Include Documentation:** Keep relevant project documentation, such as notes or settings, along with archived files for future reference.

## 4. File Management and Optimization:

- **File Size Management:**
    - **Compression:** Use compression techniques or codecs to manage file sizes without compromising quality.
    - **Resolution Adjustment:** Export in appropriate resolutions to avoid unnecessarily large files for specific uses.

- **File Formats:**
  - ○ **Choose Appropriate Formats:** Select formats that balance quality and compatibility for your intended use (e.g., H.264 for web, ProRes for high-quality archival).

- **Metadata and Tags:**
  - ○ **Add Metadata:** Include metadata and tags to make files easily searchable and identifiable (e.g., project details, author, date).

## 5. Review and Quality Control:

- **Quality Check:**
  - ○ **Verify Output:** Review output files to ensure they meet quality standards and playback as expected.
  - ○ **Test on Multiple Devices:** Test files on different devices or platforms to confirm compatibility and quality.

- **Resolve Issues:**
  - ○ **Address Problems:** If issues are found, address them promptly and re-export if necessary.

## 6. Sharing and Distribution:

- **Use Reliable Transfer Methods:**
  - ○ **File Transfer Protocols:** Use reliable methods for sharing large files, such as file transfer services (e.g., WeTransfer, Dropbox) or physical storage devices.

- **Access Control:**
  - ○ **Manage Permissions:** Set appropriate access controls and permissions for shared files to protect sensitive content.

## 7. Regular Maintenance:

- **Clean Up:** Regularly clean up old or unused files and folders to free up storage space.

- **Update Backup Protocols:** Review and update backup and archiving protocols as needed to ensure ongoing data protection.

By implementing these practices, you can ensure that your output files are well-organized, backed up, and optimized, facilitating an efficient and effective workflow.

# CHAPTER 9:
# WORKFLOW AND
# EFFICIENCY TIPS

# ORGANIZING MEDIA AND PROJECTS

E fficient organization is key to a smooth video editing workflow. Properly managing your media and project files helps you work faster and avoid potential issues. Here's a guide to organizing media and projects effectively:

1. **Setting Up a Project Structure:**

- **Create a Logical Folder Structure:**
    - **Project Root Folder:** Start with a main project folder (e.g., ProjectName/).
    - **Subfolders:** Inside the root folder, create subfolders for different types of files:
        - **/Footage/**: For raw video clips.
        - **/Audio/**: For audio files, including music and sound effects.
        - **/Graphics/**: For images, logos, and other graphic elements.
        - **/Exports/**: For rendered and final output files.
        - **/Documents/**: For project notes, scripts, and other documentation.
- **Naming Conventions:**

- ○ **Descriptive and Consistent:** Use clear and descriptive names for files and folders (e.g., Interview_JohnDoe_2024.mp4, IntroAnimation_02.psd).
- ○ **Date and Versioning:** Include dates or version numbers in filenames to track changes (e.g., ProjectName_V1_2024-07-30.mp4).

## 2. Importing and Organizing Media:

- **Use Metadata and Tags:**
  - ○ **Add Metadata:** When importing media, add relevant metadata (e.g., keywords, descriptions) to help with search and organization.
  - ○ **Tag Files:** Use tags to categorize media (e.g., B-Roll, Main Footage, Interview Clips).

- **Create Bins in Premiere Pro:**
  - ○ **Organize in Bins:** Within Adobe Premiere Pro, create bins to mirror your folder structure (e.g., Footage, Audio, Graphics).
  - ○ **Sub-Bins:** Use sub-bins for further organization (e.g., Footage/Interviews, Footage/B-Roll).

## 3. Managing Project Files:

- **Organize Sequences:**
  - ○ **Sequence Naming:** Name sequences clearly and consistently to reflect their content or purpose (e.g., Final Cut, Opening Sequence, B-Roll Compile).
  - ○ **Use Nested Sequences:** For complex projects, use nested sequences to keep timelines organized and manageable.

- **Save and Backup Regularly:**

- ○ **Frequent Saves:** Save your project frequently to avoid data loss.

- ○ **Backup:** Implement a backup system to protect against hardware failures or accidental deletions. Use cloud storage or external drives for redundancy.

## 4. Streamlining Workflow:

- **Use Keyboard Shortcuts:**
  - ○ **Customize Shortcuts:** Familiarize yourself with keyboard shortcuts for common tasks in Adobe Premiere Pro. Customize shortcuts to suit your workflow.

  - ○ **Use Presets:** Create and use presets for frequently used effects, transitions, or export settings.

- **Automate Repetitive Tasks:**
  - ○ **Batch Processing:** Use batch processing for repetitive tasks such as applying effects or exporting multiple files.

  - ○ **Adobe Media Encoder:** Utilize Adobe Media Encoder for batch exports and to streamline encoding processes.

## 5. Efficient Editing Techniques:

- **Use Proxy Files:**
  - ○ **Proxy Workflow:** Edit with lower-resolution proxy files for smoother performance, and switch to full-resolution files for final rendering.

- **Organize Your Timeline:**
  - ○ **Label Tracks:** Label and color-code video and audio tracks to keep your timeline organized.

  - ○ **Group Clips:** Use nesting or grouping to

manage multiple clips as a single entity.

## 6. Collaboration and Sharing:

- **Project Collaboration:**
    - ◦ **Shared Projects:** Use Adobe Team Projects or cloud-based services to collaborate with others on the same project.
    - ◦ **Version Control:** Maintain version control to track changes and collaborate effectively.

- **File Sharing:**
    - ◦ **Share Media and Project Files:** Use reliable file-sharing methods for distributing project files and media to team members or clients.

## 7. Regular Maintenance:

- **Clean Up Media:**
    - ◦ **Remove Unused Files:** Periodically review and delete unused media files and sequences to free up storage space.
    - ◦ **Optimize Storage:** Regularly check storage usage and optimize to ensure efficient project management.

By implementing these organizational strategies and workflow tips, you can enhance your efficiency, maintain a clear project structure, and ensure a smoother video editing process.

# KEYBOARD SHORTCUTS AND CUSTOMIZATION

**K**eyboard shortcuts can significantly enhance your efficiency and speed while working in Adobe Premiere Pro. Customizing shortcuts to fit your workflow can further streamline your editing process. Here's how to make the most of keyboard shortcuts and customize them effectively:

1. **Essential Keyboard Shortcuts:**

- **Playback Controls:**
  - **Play/Pause:** Spacebar
  - **Stop:** K
  - **Play Previous Frame:** Left Arrow
  - **Play Next Frame:** Right Arrow
  - **Play/Pause Toggle:** Shift + Spacebar

- **Editing Tools:**
  - **Selection Tool:** V
  - **Razor Tool:** C
  - **Slip Tool:** Y
  - **Roll Tool:** N

- ◦ **Trim Tool:** T
- **Timeline Navigation:**
  - ◦ **Go to In Point:** I
  - ◦ **Go to Out Point:** O
  - ◦ **Go to Previous Edit Point:** Up Arrow
  - ◦ **Go to Next Edit Point:** Down Arrow
  - ◦ **Zoom In/Out:** + (Zoom In), - (Zoom Out)
- **Cut and Paste:**
  - ◦ **Cut:** Ctrl + X (Windows) / Cmd + X (Mac)
  - ◦ **Copy:** Ctrl + C (Windows) / Cmd + C (Mac)
  - ◦ **Paste:** Ctrl + V (Windows) / Cmd + V (Mac)
- **Audio Controls:**
  - ◦ **Increase Volume:** Alt + Up Arrow (Windows) / Option + Up Arrow (Mac)
  - ◦ **Decrease Volume:** Alt + Down Arrow (Windows) / Option + Down Arrow (Mac)
  - ◦ **Mute Audio:** Shift + (Mute Toggle)

2. **Customizing Keyboard Shortcuts:**

- **Access Keyboard Shortcuts Menu:**
  - ◦ **Open Shortcut Editor:** Go to Edit > Keyboard Shortcuts (Windows) or Premiere Pro > Keyboard Shortcuts (Mac).
  - ◦ **Shortcut Editor:** The Keyboard Shortcuts dialog box will open.
- **Create or Modify Shortcuts:**
  - ◦ **Search Commands:** Use the search bar to find specific commands or tools you want to customize.
  - ◦ **Assign Shortcuts:** Click on the command you want to modify or add a shortcut to, then press

the desired key combination.

- ◦ **Remove Shortcuts:** Click the shortcut you want to remove and press Delete or Backspace.

- **Save and Export Shortcuts:**
  - ◦ **Save Customizations:** After making changes, save your custom shortcut layout by clicking OK.
  - ◦ **Export Shortcuts:** To share or backup your custom shortcuts, click on the Save As button in the Keyboard Shortcuts dialog box.

### 3. Using Preset and Default Shortcuts:

- **Import Presets:** Import keyboard shortcut presets from other users or online sources if they fit your workflow.

- **Reset to Default:** If needed, reset to Adobe's default shortcuts by selecting Restore Defaults in the Keyboard Shortcuts dialog box.

### 4. Tips for Effective Shortcut Use:

- **Consistency:** Use shortcuts consistently to build muscle memory and speed up your editing process.

- **Practice:** Regularly practice using shortcuts to become more proficient and reduce reliance on the mouse.

- **Reference Sheet:** Keep a reference sheet of commonly used shortcuts handy as you familiarize yourself with them.

### 5. Advanced Customization:

- **Macro Commands:** Use third-party tools to create macro commands if you need complex or multi-step actions.

- **Workspace Integration:** Customize shortcuts to work seamlessly with your workspace layout for a more integrated workflow.

By mastering and customizing keyboard shortcuts, you can significantly enhance your efficiency and productivity in Adobe Premiere Pro. Custom shortcuts tailored to your specific workflow will help streamline your editing process and reduce the time spent on repetitive tasks.

# USING TEMPLATES AND PRESETS

Templates and presets in Adobe Premiere Pro can save you time and ensure consistency across your projects. Here's how to effectively use and manage templates and presets:

1. **Understanding Templates and Presets:**

   - **Templates:**
     - **Definition:** Pre-designed elements such as lower thirds, titles, and transitions that you can customize for your projects.
     - **Types:** Includes title templates, motion graphics templates (MOGRTs), and sequence templates.

   - **Presets:**
     - **Definition:** Pre-configured settings for effects, transitions, and color corrections that can be applied to your clips.
     - **Types:** Includes effect presets, transition presets, and color grading presets.

2. **Using Templates:**

   - **Accessing Templates:**

- ◦ **Essential Graphics Panel:** Go to Window > Essential Graphics to access built-in motion graphics templates and create your own.
- ◦ **Adobe Stock:** Browse Adobe Stock or other sources for additional templates.

- · **Applying Templates:**
  - ◦ **Drag and Drop:** Drag templates from the Essential Graphics panel onto your timeline.
  - ◦ **Customize:** Modify text, colors, and other elements directly within the Essential Graphics panel.

- · **Creating Custom Templates:**
  - ◦ **Design:** Create your own templates using the Essential Graphics panel. Design your elements and save them as templates.
  - ◦ **Save Template:** Click on Export As Motion Graphics Template in the Essential Graphics panel to save and reuse your custom designs.

3. **Using Presets:**

- · **Accessing Presets:**
  - ◦ **Effects Panel:** Go to Window > Effects to find built-in effect presets and transition presets.
  - ◦ **Lumetri Color Panel:** Use the Lumetri Color panel for color grading presets.

- · **Applying Presets:**
  - ◦ **Drag and Drop:** Drag presets from the Effects panel onto your clips.
  - ◦ **Adjust Settings:** Modify preset settings as needed in the Effect Controls panel.

- · **Creating Custom Presets:**
  - ◦ **Apply Effects:** Configure effects and settings

on a clip to your preference.

- **Save Preset:** Click on the Effect Controls panel menu and choose Save Preset to save your customized settings for future use.

## 4. Managing Templates and Presets:

- **Organizing:**
  - **Folder Structure:** Keep templates and presets organized in specific folders within the Essential Graphics panel or Effects panel.

  - **Naming Conventions:** Use clear and descriptive names to easily identify templates and presets (e.g., LowerThirds_01, ColorGrade_Summer).

- **Importing and Exporting:**
  - **Import Templates:** Use Import in the Essential Graphics panel or File > Import to bring in new templates.

  - **Export Presets:** Save and share custom presets by right-clicking in the Effects panel and selecting Save Preset.

- **Updating:**
  - **Update Templates:** Edit existing templates to reflect new design trends or project requirements, and re-save them.

  - **Version Control:** Maintain different versions of templates and presets for various project needs.

## 5. Best Practices:

- **Consistency:** Use templates and presets to maintain consistency in style and branding across your projects.

- **Adaptation:** Customize templates and presets to suit

specific project requirements rather than using them as-is.

- **Backup:** Regularly back up your custom templates and presets to avoid data loss.

By effectively using and managing templates and presets, you can enhance your productivity, maintain a consistent style, and streamline your editing workflow in Adobe Premiere Pro.

# COLLABORATIVE WORKFLOWS

Collaborating efficiently in Adobe Premiere Pro involves managing shared projects, coordinating with team members, and maintaining workflow consistency. Here's how to set up and optimize collaborative workflows:

1. **Setting Up Collaborative Projects:**

- **Adobe Team Projects:**
  - **Definition:** A cloud-based feature that allows multiple users to work on the same project simultaneously.
  - **Setup:**
    - Go to File > New > Team Project to create a new team project.
    - Invite collaborators by sharing the project link or adding their Adobe IDs.

- **Shared Projects:**
  - **Definition:** Projects that are stored on a shared network or cloud storage where multiple users can access and edit.
  - **Setup:**
    - Store your project files and media on a

shared server or cloud storage service (e.g., Dropbox, Google Drive).

- Ensure all collaborators have access to the shared location.

## 2. Managing Media and Assets:

- **Organized Media:**
  - **Folder Structure:** Maintain a clear and consistent folder structure for media files (e.g., /Footage/, /Audio/, /Graphics/).
  - **File Naming:** Use descriptive and consistent naming conventions to avoid confusion.

- **Shared Media Libraries:**
  - **Adobe Creative Cloud Libraries:** Share assets such as colors, graphics, and logos via Adobe Creative Cloud Libraries.
  - **Access:** Collaborators can access shared libraries from the Libraries panel in Premiere Pro.

## 3. Version Control and Coordination:

- **Version Tracking:**
  - **Save Versions:** Regularly save and label different versions of your project (e.g., ProjectName_V1, ProjectName_V2).
  - **Change Logs:** Maintain a change log to track edits and updates made by different team members.

- **Communication:**
  - **Notes and Comments:** Use comments and annotations within the project or in a separate document to communicate edits and feedback.

- ○ **Regular Meetings:** Schedule regular meetings or check-ins to discuss progress and coordinate tasks.

## 4. Editing and Review Process:

- **Review and Approval:**
  - ○ **Share Previews:** Export and share preview files for feedback and review.
  - ○ **Feedback Integration:** Incorporate feedback into the project and keep track of revisions.

- **Locked Sequences:**
  - ○ **Lock Sequences:** To prevent accidental changes, lock sequences that are not currently being edited.
  - ○ **Sequence Management:** Clearly indicate which sequences are being worked on by which team member.

## 5. Handling Conflicts and Issues:

- **Conflict Resolution:**
  - ○ **Conflicting Changes:** If working on a shared project, resolve conflicts by communicating with team members to avoid overwriting each other's work.
  - ○ **Backup:** Ensure regular backups to prevent data loss in case of conflicts or errors.

- **Technical Support:**
  - ○ **Troubleshooting:** Address technical issues promptly by consulting Adobe's support resources or forums.
  - ○ **Updates:** Keep Adobe Premiere Pro and related software up to date to avoid compatibility issues.

## 6. **Optimizing Workflow:**

- **Template Use:**
    - ◦ **Shared Templates:** Create and share project templates to standardize formats and settings across the team.
    - ◦ **Presets:** Share and use effect and transition presets to maintain consistency.

- **Task Delegation:**
    - ◦ **Assign Roles:** Clearly define roles and responsibilities (e.g., editor, colorist, sound designer) to streamline workflow.
    - ◦ **Task Management:** Use project management tools (e.g., Trello, Asana) to assign tasks and track progress.

## 7. **Finalizing and Exporting:**

- **Final Review:**
    - ◦ **Final Approval:** Ensure all team members review and approve the final edit before exporting.
    - ◦ **Export Settings:** Confirm export settings match the project's requirements and deliverables.

- **Archiving Projects:**
    - ◦ **Complete Archive:** Once the project is finalized, archive all project files, media, and assets for future reference or revisions.
    - ◦ **Organize Archive:** Keep archived projects organized in a clear folder structure for easy retrieval.

By setting up an effective collaborative workflow, managing media and assets properly, and maintaining clear communication, you can ensure a smooth and efficient editing process in Adobe Premiere Pro, even with multiple team members involved.

# CHAPTER 10: TROUBLESHOOTING AND COMMON ISSUES

# RESOLVING COMMON TECHNICAL PROBLEMS

Technical issues can disrupt your editing workflow in Adobe Premiere Pro. Here's a guide to troubleshooting common problems and finding solutions:

## 1. Playback Issues:

- **Lagging or Choppy Playback:**
  - **Proxy Files:** Use proxy files for smoother playback. Go to File > Project Settings > Ingest Settings and enable proxy creation.

  - **Render Effects:** Render your timeline by selecting Sequence > Render In to Out to improve playback performance.

  - **Playback Resolution:** Lower the playback resolution from Full to 1/2 or 1/4 in the Program Monitor.

- **Black or Frozen Frames:**
  - **Media Cache:** Clear the media cache by going to Edit > Preferences > Media Cache and clicking Delete to remove cached files.

- ◦ **Update Drivers:** Ensure your graphics drivers are up to date.

## 2. **Export Problems:**

- **Failed Exports or Errors:**
  - ◦ **Check Settings:** Verify your export settings and ensure they match your project's requirements.
  - ◦ **Disk Space:** Ensure you have enough disk space for the export. Free up space if necessary.
  - ◦ **Restart:** Restart Adobe Premiere Pro and your computer to clear any temporary issues.

- **Export Quality Issues:**
  - ◦ **Codec and Format:** Ensure you are using the correct codec and format for your export. Common choices include H.264 for web and ProRes for high-quality exports.
  - ◦ **Bitrate Settings:** Adjust the bitrate settings to balance quality and file size.

## 3. **Media Import Issues:**

- **Files Not Importing:**
  - ◦ **Supported Formats:** Verify that the media files are in a supported format. Convert files to compatible formats if necessary.
  - ◦ **File Corruption:** Check if the files are corrupted by opening them in other media players or applications.

- **Missing Media:**
  - ◦ **Relink Files:** If media is missing, relink it by right-clicking on the missing file in the Project panel and selecting Link Media.

## 4. **Crashing and Performance Problems:**

- **Frequent Crashes:**
  - **Software Update:** Ensure Adobe Premiere Pro is updated to the latest version.
  - **System Requirements:** Check if your system meets the minimum requirements for running Premiere Pro.
  - **Conflict Software:** Disable or uninstall conflicting third-party plugins or software.

- **Slow Performance:**
  - **Optimize Preferences:** Adjust performance preferences by going to Edit > Preferences > Memory and allocating more RAM to Premiere Pro.
  - **Close Other Applications:** Close unnecessary applications running in the background to free up system resources.

## 5. Audio Issues:

- **No Sound:**
  - **Audio Track Mute:** Ensure that the audio track is not muted or turned down in the timeline.
  - **Audio Hardware:** Check your audio hardware settings by going to Edit > Preferences > Audio Hardware.

- **Audio Sync Problems:**
  - **Adjust Sync:** Use the Synchronize function to align audio with video. Right-click on the clips and select Synchronize.
  - **Manual Adjustment:** Adjust audio manually if synchronization is off by trimming or shifting the audio clip.

## 6. Rendering Issues:

- **Rendering Errors:**
  - **Sequence Settings:** Verify that your sequence settings match the settings of your source media.
  - **Effect Compatibility:** Check if any effects or plugins are causing rendering issues. Try disabling them and rendering again.
- **Incomplete Renders:**
  - **Render Queue:** Monitor the render queue to ensure that all items are being processed. Restart the render process if necessary.

## 7. File Compatibility Issues:

- **Unsupported Files:**
  - **Convert Files:** Use a media converter to convert unsupported file formats to a compatible format.
  - **Update Codecs:** Install necessary codecs if files are not playing properly.

## 8. General Troubleshooting Steps:

- **Reset Preferences:**
  - **Reset to Default:** To reset Adobe Premiere Pro preferences, hold Alt (Windows) / Option (Mac) while launching the application.
- **Check Adobe Forums:**
  - **Community Support:** Visit Adobe's user forums and support pages for solutions to specific issues or to seek help from other users.
- **Contact Support:**
  - **Adobe Support:** If problems persist, contact Adobe Support for assistance with unresolved issues.

By following these troubleshooting steps, you can resolve common technical problems in Adobe Premiere Pro and maintain an efficient editing workflow. Regular maintenance, updates, and good practices can help prevent many of these issues from occurring.

# PERFORMANCE OPTIMIZATION

Optimizing performance in Adobe Premiere Pro ensures smoother editing and faster rendering times. Here's a guide to enhancing your system's performance and efficiency within Premiere Pro:

1. **System Optimization:**

- **Upgrade Hardware:**
    - **RAM:** Increase the amount of RAM in your system. Adobe recommends at least 16GB, but 32GB or more is ideal for larger projects.
    - **Graphics Card:** Use a high-performance graphics card (GPU) that supports CUDA (NVIDIA) or OpenCL (AMD) for acceleration.
    - **Storage:** Use SSDs for faster read/write speeds compared to traditional hard drives. Consider a dedicated drive for media and projects.

- **System Maintenance:**
    - **Update Drivers:** Keep your graphics card and other system drivers up to date.
    - **Clean Up:** Regularly clean up your disk by removing unnecessary files and running

system maintenance tools.

- ◦ **Check for Malware:** Ensure your system is free of malware and viruses that can affect performance.

## 2. Premiere Pro Preferences:

- **Memory Allocation:**
  - ◦ **Increase RAM Allocation:** Go to Edit > Preferences > Memory and allocate more RAM to Adobe Premiere Pro while leaving enough for other applications.

- **Media Cache:**
  - ◦ **Clean Media Cache:** Go to Edit > Preferences > Media Cache and delete unused media cache files to free up space and improve performance.
  - ◦ **Cache Location:** Set the media cache to a fast drive, such as an SSD, for quicker access.

- **Playback Settings:**
  - ◦ **Playback Resolution:** Lower the playback resolution in the Program Monitor from Full to 1/2 or 1/4 to reduce processing demands.
  - ◦ **Render Previews:** Render preview files by selecting Sequence > Render In to Out to ensure smoother playback.

## 3. Project and Sequence Management:

- **Organize Projects:**
  - ◦ **Folder Structure:** Maintain a clear and organized folder structure for media files and sequences.
  - ◦ **Project Size:** Split large projects into smaller sequences or projects if performance becomes sluggish.

- **Sequence Settings:**
    - **Match Media Settings:** Ensure your sequence settings match your source media settings to avoid unnecessary scaling or processing.

## 4. Media Management:

- **Optimize Media Files:**
    - **Use Proxies:** Create proxy files for editing large high-resolution footage. Go to File > Project Settings > Ingest Settings and enable proxy creation.
    - **Transcode Media:** Transcode media to an editing-friendly format with a lower resolution or bit rate for smoother performance.

- **External Media Drives:**
    - **Fast Drives:** Use fast external drives or RAID arrays for storing and accessing media files.

## 5. Effects and Plugins:

- **Minimize Effects Usage:**
    - **Use Sparingly:** Apply effects only when necessary and avoid using too many effects simultaneously.
    - **Render Effects:** Render effects-heavy sequences by selecting Sequence > Render Effects In to Out.

- **Manage Plugins:**
    - **Update Plugins:** Ensure all installed plugins are updated to their latest versions for compatibility and performance improvements.
    - **Disable Unnecessary Plugins:** Disable or remove plugins that are not being used to

reduce processing overhead.

## 6. Background Processes:

- **Close Unnecessary Applications:**
  - **Free Resources:** Close other applications running in the background to free up system resources for Premiere Pro.

- **System Monitoring:**
  - **Task Manager/Activity Monitor:** Monitor system resource usage via Task Manager (Windows) or Activity Monitor (Mac) to identify and manage resource-heavy processes.

## 7. Regular Maintenance:

- **Update Software:**
  - **Premiere Pro Updates:** Keep Adobe Premiere Pro up to date with the latest patches and updates for performance improvements and bug fixes.

- **Backup Projects:**
  - **Frequent Backups:** Regularly back up your projects and media files to avoid data loss and ensure smooth recovery in case of system issues.

## 8. Rendering Optimization:

- **Use GPU Acceleration:**
  - **Enable GPU Acceleration:** Go to File > Project Settings > General and select Mercury Playback Engine GPU Acceleration for faster rendering.

- **Export Settings:**
  - **Optimize Settings:** Choose export settings that balance quality and performance. Adjust the bitrate and format to suit your needs.

By implementing these performance optimization strategies, you can enhance the efficiency of Adobe Premiere Pro, improve editing speed, and reduce the likelihood of technical issues impacting your workflow.

# RECOVERING
# UNSAVED PROJECTS

Recovering unsaved projects in Adobe Premiere Pro can be critical if the application crashes or if you accidentally close a project without saving. Here's a step-by-step guide to help you recover unsaved work:

1. **Auto-Save Feature:**

- **Auto-Save Settings:**
  - **Check Settings:** Ensure Auto-Save is enabled by going to Edit > Preferences > Auto Save (Windows) or Premiere Pro > Preferences > Auto Save (Mac). Verify the settings for how often Auto-Save occurs and how many versions are kept.

- **Locate Auto-Save Files:**
  - **Auto-Save Folder:** Auto-Save files are stored in a specific folder. By default, it is located in your project's directory under Premiere Pro Auto-Save.
    - **Windows:** Documents > Adobe > Premiere Pro > [version number] > Adobe Premiere Pro Auto-Save
    - **Mac:** Users/[username]/Documents/

Adobe/Premiere Pro/[version number]/Adobe Premiere Pro Auto-Save

- ◦ **Open Auto-Save Files:** Navigate to the Auto-Save folder, find the most recent version of your project, and open it in Premiere Pro.

## 2. Project Recovery:

- • **Recover from Auto-Save:**
  - ◦ **Open Auto-Save:** If Premiere Pro crashes, it will prompt you to recover the last Auto-Saved project upon reopening. Follow the prompts to open the recovered version.
  - ◦ **Manually Open:** If you need to manually open an Auto-Save file, go to File > Open Project, navigate to the Auto-Save folder, and select the appropriate file.

- • **Check for Temporary Files:**
  - ◦ **Temporary Folder:** Sometimes temporary files are created during editing. Check your system's temporary folder for any project files that might be recoverable.
    - ▪ **Windows:** C:\Users\[username]\AppData\Local\Temp
    - ▪ **Mac:** ~/Library/Application Support/Adobe/Premiere Pro/[version number]/Media Cache Files

## 3. Project Backup:

- • **Backup Regularly:**
  - ◦ **Manual Backup:** Regularly save and back up your project manually to avoid losing significant progress. Use File > Save As to create multiple versions of your project.

- **External Storage:**
  - ○ **Cloud Backup:** Consider using cloud storage services like Adobe Creative Cloud, Google Drive, or Dropbox for additional backups of your projects and media files.

## 4. Adobe Creative Cloud Sync:

- **Sync Projects:**
  - ○ **Enable Sync:** If using Adobe Creative Cloud, ensure that your projects are synced to the cloud. This can provide an additional layer of backup and recovery.

## 5. Troubleshooting Issues:

- **Check Recent Files:**
  - ○ **Open Recent Projects:** Go to File > Open Recent to see if your project is listed and open it from there.

- **Consult Adobe Support:**
  - ○ **Technical Help:** If you cannot recover your project through the above methods, consider reaching out to Adobe Support for further assistance.

By following these steps, you can increase your chances of recovering unsaved or lost projects and minimize the impact of unexpected issues or crashes in Adobe Premiere Pro. Regular saving and backups are key to protecting your work.

# CHAPTER 11: REAL-WORLD PROJECT EXAMPLES

# STEP-BY-
# STEP PROJECT
# WALKTHROUGHS

This chapter provides practical examples of real-world projects to illustrate key techniques and workflows in Adobe Premiere Pro. Each walkthrough will guide you through the process of completing a specific type of project, showcasing different features and skills.

## 1. Creating a Promotional Video

- **Objective:** Produce a 60-second promotional video for a product or service.

**Step-by-Step:**

- **Project Setup:**
    - **Create a New Project:** Open Adobe Premiere Pro and create a new project. Name it "Promotional Video."
    - **Import Media:** Import your video clips, images, and audio files into the Project panel.
- **Timeline Assembly:**
    - **Create a Sequence:** Set up a new sequence with

appropriate settings (e.g., 1920x1080, 30fps).

- **Add Clips:** Drag and drop video clips and images onto the timeline, arranging them in a logical sequence.

- **Editing:**
    - **Cutting and Trimming:** Use the Razor tool to cut clips and trim unnecessary parts.
    - **Add Transitions:** Apply basic transitions between clips for smooth visual flow.
    - **Overlay Text:** Add text overlays with key product information and promotional messages.

- **Audio:**
    - **Background Music:** Import and place background music on the audio track. Adjust levels and fade in/out as needed.
    - **Voiceovers:** Add voiceover narration if required. Sync the voiceover with the video content.

- **Final Touches:**
    - **Apply Effects:** Use video effects to enhance the visual appeal, such as color correction or filters.
    - **Export:** Export the video using settings optimized for social media or web upload (e.g., H.264 format).

---

## 2. Editing a Short Film

- **Objective:** Edit a 10-minute short film, including color correction and sound design.

**Step-by-Step:**

- **Project Setup:**
  - **Create a New Project:** Name it "Short Film."
  - **Import Media:** Import all footage, sound effects, and music files.

- **Timeline Assembly:**
  - **Create a Sequence:** Set up a sequence with the film's resolution and frame rate.
  - **Assemble Footage:** Arrange the footage on the timeline according to the film's storyboard or script.

- **Editing:**
  - **Cut and Trim:** Use cutting tools to refine the film's pacing. Remove any unnecessary scenes or bloopers.
  - **Add B-Roll:** Integrate additional footage or B-roll to enhance storytelling and cover any rough edits.

- **Color Correction:**
  - **Basic Correction:** Use the Lumetri Color panel for primary color correction (exposure, contrast, white balance).
  - **Color Grading:** Apply color grading to set the film's mood and style.

- **Sound Design:**
  - **Audio Editing:** Sync dialogue, add sound effects, and adjust audio levels.
  - **Mixing:** Use the Audio Track Mixer to balance audio levels and ensure clarity.

- **Final Touches:**
  - **Add Titles and Credits:** Create and position opening and closing titles, including credits.

- **Export:** Export the final cut with settings suitable for film festivals or digital distribution.

---

## 3. Creating a YouTube Vlog

- **Objective:** Edit a 5-minute YouTube vlog, focusing on engaging content and quick edits.

**Step-by-Step:**

- **Project Setup:**
    - **Create a New Project:** Title it "YouTube Vlog."
    - **Import Media:** Import video clips, intro music, and any graphics.

- **Timeline Assembly:**
    - **Create a Sequence:** Set up a sequence with YouTube's standard resolution (1920x1080).
    - **Place Clips:** Arrange your vlog clips on the timeline. Add intro and outro clips as needed.

- **Editing:**
    - **Cutting and Trimming:** Edit out pauses and mistakes to keep the video engaging. Use jump cuts to maintain pace.
    - **Add Graphics:** Insert lower-thirds or pop-up text to emphasize key points.

- **Audio:**
    - **Background Music:** Add upbeat background music, ensuring it doesn't overpower the dialogue.
    - **Voice Enhancement:** Apply audio effects to enhance voice clarity and reduce background noise.

- **Final Touches:**

- **Effects and Transitions:** Use simple transitions and effects to add a dynamic feel.
- **Export:** Export using YouTube's recommended settings (e.g., H.264 codec).

---

## 4. Editing a Corporate Training Video

- **Objective:** Produce a 15-minute training video with clear visuals and informative content.

### Step-by-Step:

- **Project Setup:**
  - **Create a New Project:** Name it "Corporate Training."
  - **Import Media:** Import instructional videos, slides, and voiceovers.

- **Timeline Assembly:**
  - **Create a Sequence:** Set up a sequence matching the video's resolution and frame rate.
  - **Place Media:** Arrange instructional videos, slides, and voiceovers on the timeline.

- **Editing:**
  - **Cut and Trim:** Edit out unnecessary segments and ensure a smooth flow of information.
  - **Insert Slides:** Add slides or graphics to emphasize key points or steps.

- **Audio:**
  - **Voiceovers:** Sync and adjust voiceover narration to match the video content.
  - **Background Music:** Use subtle background music to keep the video engaging without distracting from the content.

- **Final Touches:**
  - **Add Titles and Callouts:** Create titles and callout graphics for important information.
  - **Export:** Export with settings suitable for corporate training platforms (e.g., MP4 format).

These real-world project examples cover a range of scenarios you might encounter in video editing. By following these step-by-step guides, you can apply your skills to create professional-quality videos across different formats and purposes.

# CASE STUDIES OF DIFFERENT VIDEO TYPES

I n this chapter, we explore case studies of various video types, including vlogs, short films, and documentaries. Each case study provides insight into the unique editing approaches and challenges associated with these formats.

## 1. Vlogs

**Case Study: "Travel Vlog: Exploring Paris"**

- **Objective:** Create an engaging and dynamic travel vlog documenting a trip to Paris.

- **Key Elements:**
    - **Visual Style:** Use a mix of wide shots, close-ups, and point-of-view shots to capture the essence of the location.

    - **Pacing:** Maintain a fast-paced, energetic style to keep the audience engaged. Use jump cuts to eliminate long or dull segments.

    - **Audio:** Incorporate upbeat background music and on-the-go commentary. Ensure background music is balanced so it doesn't overpower the voiceover.

- ◦ **Graphics:** Add lower-thirds to introduce locations and pop-up text to highlight interesting facts.

- **Editing Techniques:**
  - ◦ **Cutting and Trimming:** Trim out repetitive or irrelevant footage to keep the video concise.
  - ◦ **Transitions:** Use smooth transitions between scenes to maintain flow. Consider creative transitions for a more dynamic feel.
  - ◦ **Color Correction:** Apply vibrant color grading to enhance the visual appeal of travel footage.

- **Challenges:**
  - ◦ **Maintaining Engagement:** Balance between showing beautiful visuals and keeping the narrative engaging.
  - ◦ **Audio Clarity:** Managing background noise and ensuring clear voiceover in busy or noisy environments.

## 2. Short Films

## Case Study: "The Last Goodbye"

- **Objective:** Edit a 10-minute drama short film focusing on emotional storytelling and visual aesthetics.

- **Key Elements:**
  - ◦ **Narrative Structure:** Ensure the story flows logically with a clear beginning, middle, and end. Maintain dramatic pacing to build tension and resolve conflict.
  - ◦ **Visual Style:** Utilize cinematic shots and maintain consistency in color grading to

match the film's tone.

- **Audio:** Use a combination of dialogue, sound effects, and a soundtrack to enhance the emotional impact.

- **Editing Techniques:**
  - **Cutting and Trimming:** Use precise cuts to enhance dramatic effect and pacing. Focus on the rhythm of the film.
  - **Color Grading:** Apply a specific color grade to set the mood and create a cohesive look across scenes.
  - **Sound Design:** Layer sound effects and music to support the narrative and add depth to scenes.

- **Challenges:**
  - **Maintaining Continuity:** Ensure visual and audio continuity throughout the film to avoid jarring changes.
  - **Emotional Impact:** Fine-tuning edits to ensure emotional beats hit effectively and the story resonates with the audience.

---

## 3. Documentaries

### Case Study: "The Forgotten Tribe"

- **Objective:** Produce a 30-minute documentary exploring the culture and challenges of a remote indigenous tribe.

- **Key Elements:**
  - **Research and Structure:** Organize the documentary into clear segments, each addressing different aspects of the tribe's life. Use interviews, B-roll, and narration to

support the storytelling.

- **Visual Style:** Incorporate a mix of interview footage, on-location shots, and historical imagery to provide a comprehensive view.

- **Audio:** Use interviews, ambient sounds, and a carefully chosen soundtrack to enhance the narrative.

- **Editing Techniques:**
  - **B-Roll Integration:** Use B-roll footage to provide context and break up interviews or talking-head segments.

  - **Narration:** Record and integrate voiceover narration to provide background information and guide the viewer through the story.

  - **Fact-Checking:** Ensure all factual information is accurate and appropriately sourced.

- **Challenges:**
  - **Sensitive Content:** Handle cultural and sensitive content with respect and accuracy, avoiding misrepresentation.

  - **Flow and Engagement:** Maintain viewer engagement by balancing informative content with compelling visuals and storytelling.

---

These case studies illustrate how different video types require tailored editing approaches to effectively communicate their intended message and engage their audience. By analyzing these examples, you can better understand how to apply editing techniques to various formats and achieve professional results.

# CHAPTER 12: STAYING CURRENT AND ADVANCED TECHNIQUES

# KEEPING UP WITH SOFTWARE UPDATES

In the rapidly evolving field of video editing, staying current with Adobe Premiere Pro updates and advancements is crucial for maintaining an efficient workflow and utilizing the latest features. This chapter provides strategies for keeping up-to-date and leveraging new advancements to enhance your editing skills.

## 1. Understanding the Importance of Updates

- **Performance Improvements:**
    - **Bug Fixes:** Updates often include fixes for bugs and glitches that can affect stability and performance.
    - **Speed Enhancements:** New versions may offer optimizations that improve rendering speeds and overall responsiveness.

- **New Features:**
    - **Enhanced Tools:** Updates may introduce new editing tools, effects, or functionalities that can enhance your workflow.
    - **Integration:** Improved integration with other Adobe Creative Cloud applications and third-

party plugins.

- **Security Updates:**
    - **Protecting Your Work:** Regular updates help protect against vulnerabilities and ensure your software is secure.

## 2. Finding and Installing Updates

- **Adobe Creative Cloud Desktop App:**
    - **Check for Updates:** Open the Creative Cloud desktop app, go to the Apps tab, and look for available updates for Premiere Pro.
    - **Automatic Updates:** Enable automatic updates to receive new versions as they are released without manual intervention.

- **Adobe Website:**
    - **Release Notes:** Visit the Adobe Premiere Pro page on the Adobe website for detailed release notes and information on new features.
    - **Manual Installation:** Download and install updates manually if needed by following instructions provided on Adobe's website.

## 3. Exploring New Features

- **Release Notes and Documentation:**
    - **Review Documentation:** Read the release notes and official documentation to understand the new features and changes in each update.
    - **Watch Tutorials:** Check out Adobe's tutorials and webinars for demonstrations of new tools and functionalities.

- **Community Forums:**

- **User Feedback:** Engage with community forums and discussion boards to learn about new features from other users' experiences and tips.

## 4. Training and Skill Development

- **Online Courses and Tutorials:**
  - **Stay Educated:** Enroll in online courses or watch tutorials that cover new features and advanced techniques in Premiere Pro.
  - **Skill Development:** Focus on areas like advanced color grading, complex transitions, or integration with After Effects.

- **Certifications:**
  - **Professional Credentials:** Consider pursuing Adobe Certified Expert (ACE) certification to validate your expertise and stay current with industry standards.

## 5. Experimenting with Advanced Techniques

- **New Effects and Tools:**
  - **Hands-On Practice:** Experiment with new effects, transitions, and tools introduced in recent updates to understand their potential applications.
  - **Innovative Techniques:** Explore creative techniques like advanced keyframing, motion graphics, or 360-degree video editing.

- **Third-Party Plugins:**
  - **Integrate Plugins:** Try out new third-party plugins that are compatible with the latest version of Premiere Pro to expand your editing capabilities.

- **Custom Workflows:**
  - ◦ **Optimize Efficiency:** Develop custom workflows and shortcuts that take advantage of new features and streamline your editing process.

## 6. Backup and Compatibility

- **Backup Projects:**
  - ◦ **Save Versions:** Regularly back up your projects and consider saving versions before updating to avoid compatibility issues.
  - ◦ **Test Updates:** Test updates on a smaller project or a copy of your main project to ensure compatibility before applying them to critical work.

- **Compatibility Checks:**
  - ◦ **Project Files:** Verify that your existing projects and media files remain compatible with the new version of Premiere Pro.
  - ◦ **Plugins and Extensions:** Check that any third-party plugins or extensions you use are updated and compatible with the latest software version.

## 7. Staying Connected

- **Adobe Blog and Newsletters:**
  - ◦ **Subscribe:** Follow the Adobe blog and subscribe to newsletters for updates on new features, tips, and industry news.

- **Professional Networks:**
  - ◦ **Join Groups:** Participate in professional networks and social media groups dedicated to video editing and Adobe Premiere Pro for

insights and updates from peers.

By actively keeping up with Adobe Premiere Pro updates and exploring new features, you can maintain a competitive edge in video editing and continuously enhance your skills. Staying informed and adapting to advancements ensures you leverage the full potential of the software and stay ahead in the ever-evolving field of video production.

# EXPLORING
# NEW FEATURES
# AND TOOLS

Adobe Premiere Pro regularly introduces new features and tools that enhance functionality and streamline editing workflows. This section will guide you on how to effectively explore and integrate these advancements into your editing practice.

## 1. Understanding New Features

- **Release Notes:**
    - **Review Updates:** Read the release notes for each new version to understand the changes and new features introduced. Adobe provides detailed documentation on new capabilities, bug fixes, and performance improvements.

    - **Highlight Key Features:** Identify features relevant to your editing needs, such as enhanced color grading tools, new effects, or improved performance.

- **Feature Previews:**
    - **Adobe Blog and Videos:** Watch Adobe's

promotional videos and blog posts for previews of new features. These resources often include demonstrations and use cases.

- **Webinars and Tutorials:** Attend Adobe webinars and tutorials to see new features in action and learn how to apply them effectively.

## 2. Experimenting with New Tools

- **Hands-On Practice:**
  - **Create Test Projects:** Start a test project to experiment with new tools and features without risking your primary projects. This allows you to explore capabilities in a risk-free environment.
  - **Apply New Effects:** Experiment with new effects and transitions on sample footage to understand their impact and creative possibilities.

- **Feature Integration:**
  - **Blend New Tools:** Integrate new tools into your existing workflows. For instance, use new color grading tools in combination with established techniques to enhance your video projects.
  - **Customize Workspaces:** Adapt your workspace layout to include new tools and panels, making them easily accessible during your editing process.

## 3. Advanced Techniques with New Features

- **Keyframing and Animation:**
  - **Explore Advanced Keyframing:** New updates may include enhanced keyframing options for

more precise animation control. Practice using these features to create complex animations and effects.

- ○ **Dynamic Animation:** Use new tools to create dynamic animations and motion graphics that enhance the visual appeal of your videos.

- **Color Grading and Effects:**
  - ○ **Advanced Color Tools:** Take advantage of advanced color grading tools for more refined control over your video's look. Experiment with new color grading features to achieve cinematic effects.

  - ○ **Custom Effects:** Utilize new effects and presets to create unique looks and styles. Explore how these effects can be customized and combined to fit your project's needs.

## 4. Learning and Adapting

- **Online Resources:**
  - ○ **Tutorials and Courses:** Follow online tutorials and courses focused on new features and advanced techniques. Platforms like Adobe's own learning hub, YouTube, and educational websites offer valuable insights.

  - ○ **Community Forums:** Engage with online forums and user groups to share experiences and tips about new features. Learn from the community's practical applications and problem-solving approaches.

- **Professional Development:**
  - ○ **Certifications and Training:** Consider advanced training or certifications to deepen your understanding of new features and

advanced editing techniques. Adobe offers certification programs that validate your skills and knowledge.

## 5. Integrating New Features into Your Workflow

- **Workflow Optimization:**
  - ◦ **Efficiency Gains:** Identify how new features can improve efficiency in your workflow. For example, new automation tools may speed up repetitive tasks or enhance collaboration.

  - ◦ **Custom Shortcuts:** Create custom shortcuts for new tools and features to streamline your editing process and enhance productivity.

- **Project Enhancement:**
  - ◦ **Update Projects:** Apply new features to existing projects to enhance their quality. For example, use improved color grading tools to regrade older footage or new effects to add a fresh look.

  - ◦ **Innovative Projects:** Start new projects that specifically leverage the latest features, exploring creative possibilities and pushing the boundaries of your editing skills.

## 6. Feedback and Improvement

- **User Feedback:**
  - ◦ **Provide Feedback:** Share your feedback with Adobe through their user forums or feedback channels. Your input helps shape future updates and improvements.

  - ◦ **Stay Informed:** Regularly check for updates and enhancements to stay current with the latest advancements in Adobe Premiere Pro.

- **Continuous Learning:**
  - **Adapt to Changes:** Keep adapting your skills and workflows as new features are introduced. Continuously learning and integrating new tools ensures you remain at the forefront of video editing technology.

By proactively exploring and integrating new features and tools in Adobe Premiere Pro, you can enhance your editing capabilities and stay competitive in the field. Regular experimentation and adaptation to updates will help you leverage the latest advancements to create high-quality, innovative video content.

## Chapter 12: Staying Current and Advanced Techniques

### Advanced Techniques and Industry Trends

As the video editing landscape evolves, mastering advanced techniques and staying informed about industry trends are essential for creating cutting-edge content. This section explores advanced editing methods and current trends shaping the industry.

### 1. Advanced Editing Techniques

- **Multi-Cam Editing:**
  - **Setup and Sync:** Use multi-camera editing features to synchronize and edit footage from multiple cameras. Learn to create and switch between camera angles seamlessly.
  - **Live Switching:** Utilize live switching options for real-time previews and adjustments, especially useful in live event editing.
- **Advanced Color Grading:**
  - **Color Wheels and Curves:** Utilize advanced color wheels and curves for precise color

adjustments and grading. Experiment with color matching tools to ensure consistency across shots.

- **Selective Color Correction:** Apply color correction to specific areas of your footage to enhance or alter colors selectively.

- **Dynamic Motion Graphics:**
  - **Motion Graphics Templates:** Create and customize motion graphics templates for dynamic and professional-looking animations.

  - **Advanced Keyframing:** Use advanced keyframing techniques for smooth and complex animations, including 3D animations and tracking.

- **Complex Transitions and Effects:**
  - **Custom Transitions:** Design and apply custom transitions to add a unique touch to your videos. Combine multiple effects to create complex transitions.

  - **Advanced Effects:** Explore advanced effects like particle systems, chroma keying, and 3D rendering to create visually compelling content.

- **Sound Design and Mixing:**
  - **Surround Sound Mixing:** Incorporate surround sound mixing techniques for immersive audio experiences. Use advanced audio effects and panning to create a 3D soundscape.

  - **Audio Restoration:** Apply advanced audio restoration techniques to clean up and enhance dialogue or soundtrack quality.

## 2. Industry Trends

- **AI and Machine Learning:**
    - **Automated Editing:** Leverage AI-powered tools for automated editing tasks, such as scene detection, content-aware fill, and smart cropping.
    - **Enhanced Effects:** Use AI to apply effects and color grading automatically based on content analysis, saving time and improving efficiency.

- **Virtual Reality (VR) and Augmented Reality (AR):**
    - **360-Degree Video:** Create and edit 360-degree videos for immersive VR experiences. Use specialized tools for stitching and editing panoramic footage.
    - **AR Integration:** Integrate AR elements into videos, such as interactive graphics and real-time data overlays, to engage viewers in new ways.

- **Cloud-Based Collaboration:**
    - **Remote Editing:** Utilize cloud-based collaboration tools for remote editing and review. Share projects and receive feedback in real time from team members around the world.
    - **Version Control:** Implement version control systems to manage project changes and revisions effectively.

- **High Dynamic Range (HDR):**
    - **HDR Content Creation:** Produce and edit HDR content for enhanced color and contrast. Use HDR tools to ensure accurate color

representation and dynamic range.

- ◦ **Delivery Standards:** Follow industry standards for HDR delivery, including format specifications and color grading practices.

- **Short-Form Content and Social Media:**
  - ◦ **Vertical Videos:** Edit vertical videos optimized for social media platforms like Instagram and TikTok. Utilize tools for easy trimming and formatting for mobile screens.

  - ◦ **Engagement Metrics:** Focus on editing techniques that maximize viewer engagement, such as quick cuts, captions, and eye-catching visuals.

- **Data-Driven Storytelling:**
  - ◦ **Infographics and Data Visualization:** Integrate infographics and data visualizations into videos to present complex information clearly and attractively.

  - ◦ **Interactive Content:** Develop interactive video content that allows viewers to choose their own path or explore additional information.

## 3. Implementing Advanced Techniques

- **Experiment and Practice:**
  - ◦ **Create Test Projects:** Use test projects to experiment with advanced techniques and trends before applying them to client or personal work.

  - ◦ **Build Skills:** Continuously build your skills through practice and learning. Engage with online communities and resources to stay updated.

- **Integrate Trends:**
    - **Adapt Content:** Adapt your content strategy to incorporate industry trends, ensuring your work remains relevant and innovative.
    - **Update Workflows:** Update your workflows and toolsets to leverage new technologies and trends effectively.

- **Professional Development:**
    - **Attend Workshops and Conferences:** Participate in industry workshops, conferences, and events to learn about the latest advancements and network with professionals.
    - **Certifications:** Pursue advanced certifications and training programs to validate your expertise and stay current with industry standards.

---

By mastering advanced techniques and staying informed about industry trends, you can push the boundaries of your editing skills and remain at the forefront of the video editing field. Embrace new technologies, continuously refine your techniques, and adapt to emerging trends to create innovative and engaging content.

# ADVANCED TECHNIQUES AND INDUSTRY TRENDS

This chapter focuses on sophisticated editing techniques and emerging trends in the video editing industry. By exploring these aspects, you'll be equipped to enhance your skills and stay relevant in a rapidly evolving field.

## 1. Advanced Editing Techniques

- **Multi-Camera Editing:**
  - **Setup and Synchronization:** Learn to set up multi-camera sequences and synchronize footage using timecode, audio waveforms, or manual alignment.

  - **Angle Switching:** Utilize Premiere Pro's multi-camera tools to switch between different angles in real time during editing, allowing for dynamic storytelling.

- **Complex Color Grading:**
  - **Lumetri Color Panel:** Dive deeper into advanced features of the Lumetri Color panel, such as color wheels, curves, and HSL

secondary color correction for precise color grading.

- **Creative LUTs:** Create and apply custom Look-Up Tables (LUTs) for unique color grading styles and ensure consistency across projects.

- **Motion Graphics and Animation:**
    - **Advanced Keyframing:** Master advanced keyframing techniques to create intricate animations and transitions. Experiment with bezier handles and easing options for smoother animations.

    - **Essential Graphics Panel:** Utilize the Essential Graphics panel for creating and animating complex motion graphics and text layers.

- **Audio Post-Production:**
    - **Advanced Audio Effects:** Apply advanced audio effects and plugins for noise reduction, dynamic range compression, and spatial audio processing.

    - **Audio Mixing:** Use tools like the Audio Track Mixer to balance levels, create audio submixes, and apply effects in a mix environment.

- **3D Editing and Effects:**
    - **3D Camera:** Incorporate 3D camera movement and layers to create depth and perspective in your projects.

    - **3D Effects and Compositing:** Use 3D effects and compositing techniques to integrate 3D elements and enhance visual storytelling.

## 2. Industry Trends

- **Artificial Intelligence (AI) and Machine Learning:**

- **Automated Editing:** Explore AI-powered features for automated tasks such as scene detection, auto-reframing for social media formats, and intelligent content tagging.

- **Enhanced Search and Organization:** Use AI to enhance media management through advanced search capabilities and automated metadata tagging.

- **Virtual Reality (VR) and Augmented Reality (AR):**
  - **360-Degree Video Editing:** Learn techniques for editing 360-degree videos, including stitching, spatial audio, and VR-specific effects.

  - **AR Integration:** Create AR experiences by integrating interactive elements and overlays that enhance viewer engagement.

- **Cloud-Based Collaboration:**
  - **Remote Editing:** Utilize cloud-based platforms for collaborative editing and project management, enabling real-time feedback and updates.

  - **Version Control:** Implement version control systems to track changes and manage project versions effectively.

- **High Dynamic Range (HDR):**
  - **HDR Workflow:** Incorporate HDR techniques to enhance video quality with greater contrast and color depth. Ensure proper calibration and delivery standards for HDR content.

  - **Delivery Standards:** Adhere to industry standards for HDR formats and metadata to ensure compatibility across different playback devices.

- **Short-Form and Social Media Content:**
  - **Vertical and Square Formats:** Optimize content for social media platforms with vertical and square formats, utilizing tools for efficient cropping and formatting.
  - **Engagement Strategies:** Implement strategies to boost engagement, such as quick cuts, captions, and interactive elements.

- **Data-Driven Content:**
  - **Infographics and Data Visualization:** Integrate infographics and data visualizations into your videos to present complex information clearly and attractively.
  - **Interactive Video:** Develop interactive video content that allows viewers to make choices or explore additional content.

## 3. Implementing Advanced Techniques

- **Practice and Experimentation:**
  - **Test Projects:** Create test projects to explore advanced techniques and trends before applying them to client work or final projects.
  - **Experiment:** Continuously experiment with new tools and techniques to understand their capabilities and applications.

- **Adapting Workflows:**
  - **Integration:** Integrate new techniques and tools into your existing workflows to enhance efficiency and creativity.
  - **Customization:** Customize your editing environment to incorporate advanced tools and streamline your editing process.

- **Professional Development:**
  - ◦ **Continuous Learning:** Stay updated with industry trends and advancements through online courses, tutorials, and professional workshops.
  - ◦ **Networking:** Engage with the editing community through forums, social media, and industry events to share knowledge and stay informed.

---

By mastering advanced techniques and staying abreast of industry trends, you can enhance your video editing skills and remain competitive in a dynamic field. Embrace innovation, continuously refine your craft, and leverage new technologies to produce exceptional content.

# APPENDICES

# GLOSSARY OF TERMS

This glossary provides definitions for key terms and concepts used throughout the guide. Familiarity with these terms will help you better understand Adobe Premiere Pro's features and video editing techniques.

**A**

- **Aspect Ratio:** The ratio of the width to the height of a video frame. Common aspect ratios include 16:9 (widescreen) and 4:3 (standard).

- **Audio Mixer:** A tool in Premiere Pro used to adjust and balance audio levels, apply effects, and create submixes.

- **Alpha Channel:** A channel in an image or video that represents transparency. It controls which parts of the image are visible or hidden.

**B**

- **Backups:** Copies of project files or media used to prevent data loss. Regular backups ensure that work is not lost due to system failures or errors.

- **B-Roll:** Supplementary footage used to enrich the main

narrative or cover cuts in the primary footage.

## C

- **Chroma Key:** A technique used to remove a specific color (usually green or blue) from a video to replace it with another image or video.

- **Color Correction:** The process of adjusting colors in a video to achieve a desired look or correct color imbalances.

- **Composition:** The arrangement of visual elements in a video frame, including framing, positioning, and layering of clips and graphics.

## D

- **Dynamic Link:** A feature that allows you to seamlessly integrate and edit assets between Adobe Premiere Pro and other Adobe Creative Cloud applications like After Effects.

- **Duration:** The length of a clip or sequence from start to finish.

## E

- **Effect Controls Panel:** The panel in Premiere Pro where you can adjust the properties and settings of applied effects.

- **Essential Graphics Panel:** A panel for creating and editing text, titles, and motion graphics.

## F

- **Frame Rate:** The number of frames displayed per

second in a video. Common frame rates include 24fps (film), 30fps (television), and 60fps (high frame rate).

- **Footage:** Raw video clips or sequences captured by a camera or imported into a project.

## G

- **GPU Acceleration:** Utilizes the graphics processing unit to accelerate rendering and playback performance in Premiere Pro.

- **Green Screen:** A chroma keying technique where a green background is removed to replace it with another video or image.

## H

- **Hue:** A color attribute that defines the color itself, such as red, green, or blue.

- **High Dynamic Range (HDR):** A video format that provides a wider range of colors and contrast, offering more vivid and realistic images.

## I

- **Importing:** The process of bringing media files into a Premiere Pro project from external sources.

- **In and Out Points:** Markers used to define the start (In) and end (Out) points of a clip or sequence.

## J

- **J-Cut:** An editing technique where the audio from the next scene starts before the visual cut, creating a smoother transition between scenes.

- **Jump Cut:** A sudden and noticeable cut between shots that creates a jarring effect or fast-paced feel.

## K

- **Keyframes:** Markers used to define changes in properties over time, such as position, scale, or opacity, allowing for animations and effects.

## L

- **LUT (Look-Up Table):** A preset color grading tool used to apply specific color corrections or creative looks to footage.
- **Lumetri Color Panel:** A color grading and correction tool in Premiere Pro that allows for detailed adjustments to color and exposure.

## M

- **Motion Graphics:** Animated graphic elements, such as text or shapes, that are used to enhance video content.
- **Multi-Camera Editing:** A feature that allows you to edit footage from multiple camera angles simultaneously.

## N

- **Nest:** The process of grouping multiple clips or sequences into a single nested sequence for easier management and editing.
- **Noise Reduction:** Techniques used to minimize unwanted background noise or audio disturbances.

## O

- **Opacity:** The degree of transparency of a clip or layer. Lower opacity makes the layer more transparent.

- **Out Point:** The end marker of a clip or sequence defining where the clip ends.

## P

- **Premiere Pro Project File:** A file that contains all the elements of a video project, including sequences, clips, and settings.

- **Proxy:** Lower-resolution versions of high-resolution footage used to improve editing performance.

## Q

- **Quality:** The overall visual or audio fidelity of a video or audio clip, which can be affected by resolution, bitrate, and compression.

## R

- **Rendering:** The process of generating the final output of a video project, including applying effects and exporting the finished product.

- **Razor Tool:** A tool used to cut or split a clip into smaller segments.

## S

- **Sequence:** A timeline within Premiere Pro that contains and arranges video and audio clips for editing.

- **Source Monitor:** A panel where you can preview and

trim clips before adding them to the timeline.

## T

- **Timeline:** The area in Premiere Pro where you arrange and edit clips, add transitions, and apply effects.
- **Trim:** Adjusting the in and out points of a clip to alter its duration and fit it into the timeline.

## U

- **Unlink:** The process of separating audio from video in a clip, allowing them to be edited independently.

## V

- **Vector Graphics:** Graphics defined by mathematical equations, allowing for scalable and resolution-independent images.
- **Video Effects:** Filters and adjustments applied to video clips to modify their appearance or add creative elements.

## W

- **Workspace:** The arrangement of panels and tools in Premiere Pro that you customize to suit your editing needs.
- **Watermark:** A visible logo or text overlay added to a video to protect copyright or brand content.

## X

- **X-axis:** The horizontal axis in video editing, used to adjust the position of elements in the frame.

## Y

- **Y-axis:** The vertical axis in video editing, used to adjust the position of elements in the frame.

## Z

- **Zoom:** The process of changing the magnification level of a video clip or timeline view, affecting how much detail is visible.

This glossary should serve as a helpful reference as you navigate Adobe Premiere Pro and its various functionalities. Understanding these terms will enhance your ability to utilize the software effectively and communicate clearly about your video editing projects.

# KEYBOARD SHORTCUTS CHEAT SHEET

**U**sing keyboard shortcuts in Adobe Premiere Pro can significantly speed up your editing process and improve efficiency. Here is a comprehensive cheat sheet of commonly used shortcuts:

## General Shortcuts

- **New Project:** Ctrl + Alt + N (Windows) / Cmd + Option + N (Mac)

- **Open Project:** Ctrl + Alt + O (Windows) / Cmd + Option + O (Mac)

- **Save Project:** Ctrl + S (Windows) / Cmd + S (Mac)

- **Undo:** Ctrl + Z (Windows) / Cmd + Z (Mac)

- **Redo:** Ctrl + Shift + Z (Windows) / Cmd + Shift + Z (Mac)

- **Close Project:** Ctrl + W (Windows) / Cmd + W (Mac)

## Timeline Navigation

- **Play/Pause:** Spacebar
- **Stop:** K
- **Go to In Point:** Shift + I
- **Go to Out Point:** Shift + O
- **Go to Next Edit Point:** Down Arrow
- **Go to Previous Edit Point:** Up Arrow
- **Move Playhead to Start:** Home (Windows) / Fn + Left Arrow (Mac)
- **Move Playhead to End:** End (Windows) / Fn + Right Arrow (Mac)
- **Zoom In Timeline:** =
- **Zoom Out Timeline:** -

## Editing Clips

- **Cut Clip:** Ctrl + K (Windows) / Cmd + K (Mac)
- **Copy Clip:** Ctrl + C (Windows) / Cmd + C (Mac)
- **Paste Clip:** Ctrl + V (Windows) / Cmd + V (Mac)
- **Delete Clip:** Delete (Windows) / Fn + Delete (Mac)
- **Ripple Delete:** Shift + Delete (Windows) / Shift + Fn + Delete (Mac)
- **Extend Edit:** Alt + ] (Windows) / Option + ] (Mac)
- **Trim Edit:** Alt + [ (Windows) / Option + [ (Mac)
- **Nudge Clip Left:** Alt + Left Arrow (Windows) / Option + Left Arrow (Mac)
- **Nudge Clip Right:** Alt + Right Arrow (Windows) / Option + Right Arrow (Mac)

## Playback Controls

- **Step Forward (One Frame):** Right Arrow
- **Step Backward (One Frame):** Left Arrow
- **Fast Forward:** L
- **Rewind:** J
- **Slow Motion Playback:** Shift + L or Shift + J

## Markers and In/Out Points

- **Add Marker:** M
- **Clear Marker:** Ctrl + Shift + M (Windows) / Cmd + Shift + M (Mac)
- **Go to Next Marker:** Shift + M
- **Go to Previous Marker:** Ctrl + Shift + M (Windows) / Cmd + Shift + M (Mac)
- **Set In Point:** I
- **Set Out Point:** O
- **Clear In Point:** Alt + I (Windows) / Option + I (Mac)
- **Clear Out Point:** Alt + O (Windows) / Option + O (Mac)

## Tools

- **Selection Tool:** V
- **Razor Tool:** C
- **Ripple Edit Tool:** B
- **Rolling Edit Tool:** N
- **Rate Stretch Tool:** R
- **Pen Tool:** P

- **Hand Tool:** H

- **Zoom Tool:** Z

## Audio Editing

- **Increase Audio Volume:** Ctrl + Shift + ↑ (Windows) / Cmd + Shift + ↑ (Mac)

- **Decrease Audio Volume:** Ctrl + Shift + ↓ (Windows) / Cmd + Shift + ↓ (Mac)

- **Toggle Audio Track Mixer:** Shift + 6

## Effects and Transitions

- **Apply Default Transition:** Ctrl + D (Windows) / Cmd + D (Mac)

- **Apply Default Audio Transition:** Ctrl + Shift + D (Windows) / Cmd + Shift + D (Mac)

- **Open Effects Controls Panel:** Shift + 5

## Export and Rendering

- **Open Export Settings:** Ctrl + M (Windows) / Cmd + M (Mac)

- **Render Effects In to Out:** Enter

- **Queue Export:** Ctrl + Alt + M (Windows) / Cmd + Option + M (Mac)

## Workspace and Panels

- **Toggle Full-Screen Mode:** Ctrl + (Windows) / Cmd + (Mac)

- **Show/Hide Program Monitor:** Shift + 1

- **Show/Hide Source Monitor:** Shift + 2

- **Show/Hide Timeline:** Shift + 3

- **Show/Hide Project Panel:** Shift + 4

- **Show/Hide Effects Panel:** Shift + 5

## Customization

- **Customize Keyboard Shortcuts:** Ctrl + Alt + K (Windows) / Cmd + Option + K (Mac)

- **Reset Workspace:** Window > Workspaces > Reset to Saved Layout

This cheat sheet includes essential shortcuts to streamline your workflow in Adobe Premiere Pro. Familiarize yourself with these shortcuts to enhance your editing efficiency and productivity.

# ADDITIONAL RESOURCES AND REFERENCES

T o further enhance your skills and knowledge in Adobe Premiere Pro, consider exploring the following resources and references:

## 1. Official Adobe Resources

- **Adobe Premiere Pro Help Center:** Comprehensive guides, tutorials, and troubleshooting tips provided by Adobe. Adobe Help Center

- **Adobe Premiere Pro User Guide:** In-depth documentation on Premiere Pro features and workflows. Adobe User Guide

## 2. Online Tutorials and Courses

- **Adobe Creative Cloud Tutorials:** Official Adobe tutorials on various Premiere Pro features and techniques. Adobe Tutorials

- **LinkedIn Learning:** Offers a range of courses from

beginner to advanced levels on Premiere Pro. LinkedIn Learning

- **Udemy:** Online courses and tutorials covering specific aspects of Premiere Pro and video editing. Udemy

- **YouTube Channels:**
  - **Adobe Creative Cloud:** Official channel with tutorials and tips. Adobe Creative Cloud on YouTube
  - **Film Riot:** Tutorials on filmmaking and editing techniques. Film Riot on YouTube
  - **Premiere Gal:** Tips, tutorials, and reviews related to Premiere Pro. Premiere Gal on YouTube

## 3. Books and Guides

- **"Adobe Premiere Pro Classroom in a Book"** by the Adobe Creative Team: A detailed guide on using Premiere Pro with hands-on projects.

- **"Adobe Premiere Pro CC: Visual QuickStart Guide"** by Lisa Fridsma and Brad Bartlett: A user-friendly guide covering essential features and workflows.

- **"The Filmmaker's Handbook"** by Steven Ascher and Edward Pincus: Comprehensive guide on filmmaking and video editing techniques.

## 4. Forums and Communities

- **Adobe Support Community:** Engage with other Premiere Pro users and Adobe experts to ask questions and share knowledge. Adobe Support Community

- **Reddit (r/premiere):** A subreddit dedicated to

Adobe Premiere Pro for discussions, advice, and troubleshooting. Reddit Premiere

- **Creative COW:** Forums and tutorials on video editing and Premiere Pro. Creative COW

## 5. Professional Associations and Certifications

- **Adobe Certified Expert (ACE):** Certification program to validate your expertise in Adobe Premiere Pro and other Adobe products. Adobe Certification

- **American Society of Media Photographers (ASMP):** Professional association offering resources and networking for media professionals. ASMP

## 6. Additional Tools and Plugins

- **Envato Elements:** Access a library of templates, effects, and stock footage for use in Premiere Pro. Envato Elements

- **Motion Array:** A marketplace for Premiere Pro templates, presets, and royalty-free assets. Motion Array

- **Filmora Effects Store:** Additional effects and transitions for enhancing your Premiere Pro projects. Filmora Effects

These resources will help you deepen your understanding of Adobe Premiere Pro and stay current with industry trends and techniques. Whether you're looking for tutorials, professional advice, or advanced tools, these references provide valuable support for mastering video editing.

# AFTERWORD

As we close this exploration of Adobe Premiere Pro, it's important to reflect on the journey we've undertaken and look ahead to the road that lies beyond. Mastering video editing is a continual process of learning, adapting, and experimenting. The skills and techniques discussed in this guide are just the beginning of a lifelong adventure in the world of video production.

The power of Adobe Premiere Pro lies not only in its vast array of features but also in its ability to adapt to the evolving needs of its users. From simple edits to complex visual effects, the software empowers you to bring your creative visions to life. As you move forward, remember that your growth as an editor will be fueled by curiosity and experimentation.

To truly excel, stay engaged with the latest industry trends and updates. Adobe frequently releases new versions with enhanced features and tools, so keeping abreast of these changes will help you stay at the forefront of video editing technology. Engage with the community of editors and creators, participate in forums, and share your work to gain valuable feedback and inspiration.

This book has aimed to be a comprehensive resource, but the field of video editing is vast and ever-changing. Continue to seek out additional learning resources, participate in online courses, and explore other editing software to broaden your perspective and refine your skills.

Thank you for choosing this guide as a companion on your journey with Adobe Premiere Pro. Your dedication to mastering this craft is commendable, and I encourage you to take the knowledge gained here and apply it creatively and confidently. Every video you edit is a new opportunity to tell a story, evoke emotions, and make an impact.

As you continue to create, may your work resonate with audiences and reflect the passion and skill you've developed. The world of video editing is rich with possibilities, and your contributions are sure to be both meaningful and inspiring.

Best of luck on your creative journey, and may your future projects be met with success and fulfillment.

— Edwin Cano

# ACKNOWLEDGEMENT

The creation of this guide would not have been possible without the support and contributions of many individuals and communities. I am deeply grateful to all those who have played a role in shaping this book.

First and foremost, I would like to thank the team at Adobe for developing Adobe Premiere Pro, a tool that has revolutionized video editing and empowered countless creators around the world. Your innovative work continues to set the standard for video editing software.

I extend my heartfelt gratitude to my colleagues and mentors who have provided invaluable insights and feedback throughout the writing process. Your expertise and encouragement have been instrumental in refining the content and ensuring its relevance and accuracy.

Special thanks to the video editing community—both online and offline. Your shared knowledge, tutorials, and forums have been a constant source of inspiration and learning. The collaborative spirit of this community has greatly influenced my approach to video editing and has enriched the content of this guide.

I would also like to acknowledge my family and friends for

their unwavering support and patience during the creation of this book. Your encouragement and understanding have been a cornerstone of this endeavor.

Lastly, to the readers of this guide, thank you for your interest and commitment to mastering Adobe Premiere Pro. It is my hope that this book will be a valuable resource as you embark on your own journey of video editing. Your enthusiasm for learning and creativity drives the heart of this project.

Thank you all for your contributions and support.

— Edwin Cano

# ABOUT THE AUTHOR

**Edwin Cano**

Edwin Cano is a seasoned video editor and content creator with extensive experience in digital media production. With a background in both creative and technical aspects of video editing, Edwin has worked on a diverse range of projects, including feature films, documentaries, corporate videos, and online content.

Edwin's journey in video editing began with a passion for storytelling and a fascination with the power of visual media. Over the years, he has honed his skills with leading editing software, including Adobe Premiere Pro, and has become adept at translating complex ideas into compelling visual narratives. His work is characterized by a keen attention to detail, innovative use of effects, and a deep understanding of both the art and science of video editing.

In addition to his professional work, Edwin is dedicated to sharing his knowledge and expertise with others. He has conducted workshops, written articles, and created tutorials aimed at helping aspiring editors and content creators enhance their skills and achieve their creative goals. His teaching approach emphasizes practical application, hands-on learning, and a supportive environment for growth.

Edwin holds a degree in Film and Media Studies and has continuously sought opportunities for professional development in the field. His commitment to staying current with industry trends and technological advancements ensures that his insights and techniques remain relevant and effective.

Through Mastering Adobe Premiere Pro, Edwin aims to provide a comprehensive and accessible resource for both novice and experienced video editors. His goal is to empower readers with the tools and knowledge needed to excel in video editing and bring their creative visions to life.

When he's not editing, Edwin enjoys exploring new media technologies, engaging with the creative community, and continuing his own journey of learning and discovery in the world of video production.

Connect with Edwin Cano
Instagram: @imceowin
Website: www.imceowin.com
Email: author@imceowin.com

# PRAISE FOR AUTHOR

*"Edwin Cano's Mastering Adobe Premiere Pro is a tour de force in video editing literature. His comprehensive and accessible approach demystifies the complexities of Premiere Pro, making it an invaluable resource for both beginners and seasoned editors. Edwin's deep understanding of the software, coupled with his practical insights, ensures that readers are well-equipped to tackle any editing challenge. A must-have for anyone serious about mastering video editing."*

*- JANE S., SENIOR VIDEO EDITOR*

*"Edwin Cano has crafted an exceptional guide with Mastering Adobe Premiere Pro. His ability to break down intricate techniques into understandable steps showcases his expertise and teaching prowess. This book is a testament to his commitment to helping others succeed in the dynamic field of video editing. Edwin's passion for the craft shines through every page, making this guide an indispensable tool for video professionals."*

*- MICHAEL J., MEDIA PRODUCTION SPECIALIST*

*"With Mastering Adobe Premiere Pro, Edwin Cano offers a clear and practical roadmap for navigating one of the most powerful*

video editing tools available. His comprehensive coverage of both basic and advanced techniques, combined with real-world examples, provides readers with a robust understanding of Premiere Pro. Edwin's expertise and dedication to the craft are evident throughout this outstanding guide."

*- SOPHIA L., CREATIVE DIRECTOR*

"Edwin Cano's guide to Adobe Premiere Pro is a game-changer for anyone looking to elevate their video editing skills. His ability to simplify complex concepts and provide actionable tips reflects his deep knowledge and experience in the field. Mastering Adobe Premiere Pro is not just a book; it's a masterclass in video editing from one of the industry's leading experts."

*- DAVID M., VIDEO PRODUCTION MANAGER*

# THANK YOU

Dear Readers,

Thank you for choosing Mastering Adobe Premiere Pro as your guide in your video editing journey. Your commitment to learning and growing in this dynamic field is truly inspiring. I am honored to have had the opportunity to share my knowledge and insights with you through this book.

Creating this guide has been a rewarding experience, and I hope it has provided you with the tools and confidence to excel in your video editing endeavors. Remember, every edit you make and every project you complete brings you closer to mastering the art of video editing.

I encourage you to continue exploring, experimenting, and pushing the boundaries of your creativity. The world of video editing is vast and full of possibilities, and your contributions will undoubtedly add to its richness and diversity.

Thank you once again for your support and for being part of this journey. Wishing you all the best in your future projects and endeavors.

Warm regards,

— Edwin Cano

www.ingramcontent.com/pod-product-compliance
Lightning Source LLC
LaVergne TN
LVHW051443050326
832903LV00030BD/3220